FIRST-TIME DAD MASTERY

Simple, Proven Strategies for Navigating
the Changes and Challenges, Emotional
Bonding, Balancing Work and Family, and
Being a Supportive Partner

DANTE A. CACAL

Contents

Introduction

Congratulations, you've become a father! How do you feel?

You might have carefully thought about having a baby and made a final decision only after months or even years. You might have prepared yourself for the moment of your child's birth in your head a thousand times. Alternatively, you might have reacted with surprise when your partner told you they were pregnant, and you were going to become a father. After the initial shock and from that moment onward, you might have gone through a constant emotional roller-coaster. One day, you might have felt incredibly confident and ready to face the unexpected challenge. The next day, you might have suddenly realized there was no turning back, and you had to put all your effort into raising your child. You might have spent days and nights wondering what will happen and if you'll be a good father. Ready or not, all the people around you felt happy for you and made you feel more secure as you went through the emotional roller-coaster every time you discussed the pregnancy. When your child was finally born, you might have gushed with happiness. It doesn't matter if you were prepared or not—I am sure you have asked yourself the fateful question: *Now what?* You might have seen your self-confidence slowly decrease while your fears prevailed. You might have felt overwhelmed by all your emotions and the need to vent to someone. Therefore, you turned to your friends who already have babies and seem to do just fine. However, the only advice you managed to receive was a simple, "It will get easier"—the most predictable and unhelpful piece of advice one could give.

You might feel like you need something more than a one-size-fits-all solution. You might understand fatherhood requires many skills, and you want to master all of them. You might want to avoid your parents' mistakes and be the perfect father for your baby. At the same time, you also realize you must face many challenges, starting from the prejudice linked with fatherhood. Until recently, society taught fathers that they didn't have to be home and help take care of their children. Conversely, they had to dedicate more to their work to provide everything their family needed. After all, their salaries were counted on to raise the children. Therefore, fathers were always expected to work more hours, late nights, and even during weekends, if possible, and be emotionally detached from their children. Obviously, they played together from time to time, but most of the work was done by mothers. Centuries of history confirm this scenario.

However, in the last decade or so, something has changed. Fathers have become more interested in providing practical and emotional support to their partners, thus making family a priority over their jobs. On one hand, this means they have built a strong and deep connection with their significant other. On the other hand, they have had to overcome many obstacles society has created. As research explains, "A first-time father's perspective may change forever the minute he gains knowledge of pregnancy as he awaits the arrival of his baby, with the potential of capturing his heart forever" (Talley, 2017). If you think you're the only father to struggle with the enormous responsibility of fatherhood, you're not, and it's time to rethink this. Nowadays, more and more fathers believe raising children alongside the other parent is essential to fostering a positive home environment and helping their babies succeed as adults. As many fathers share this belief, they also share the same struggles.

Becoming a father doesn't only imply having more responsibilities inside the family but also finding a balance between different aspects of life. First of all, the relationship with your significant other changes. Before having a baby, there were just the two of you, and you dedicated all your time to making them happy, and vice versa. Now, there's another human being that requires a lot of attention, energy, and patience. Therefore, both your partner and you dedicate most of your time to this new baby. However, you don't face the birth in the same way. In fact, your partner might undergo postpartum emotional and physical changes that you can't understand. Even if you try to be supportive, it seems like you can't do anything right. You try to encourage your partner in various ways and help them with taking care of the baby, but you feel like there's a wall between the both of you, and you don't know how to break through it. You realize there are some communication barriers between the two of you and feel helpless.

In addition to having communication issues, you also face an identity crisis. Society has always taught you to focus on your job and nothing else, while you want to dedicate yourself to your partner and baby. Therefore, you feel misunderstood and rejected, especially by some of your colleagues and superiors. Moreover, you now have to juggle three different roles: father, professional, and partner. Dedicating enough time to all of them is hard, and you feel like you won't be able to do your best in any of your roles. You must also adjust your lifestyle and routines to satisfy your baby's needs. If you've ever heard parents complain about sleepless nights, especially in the first months after childbirth, be ready because they're real, and you'll have to face them, too. You can't escape them. Finally, being a father also involves added financial pressure. As amazing as it is to finally have a baby, it also implies more expenses and planning. In fact, you want the best for your baby, so you might want to save enough money for their education and well-being. In general, you might feel unprepared and overwhelmed. No matter how many books, blogs, or forums you have checked, or how many friends you've asked for help— you feel like you can't handle everything. And it only makes you feel more overwhelmed and anxious.

Some time ago, I found myself in the same situation. I have four children, so I've experienced all the challenges related to father-hood. I also have a full-time corporate job; thus, balancing work and life hasn't been easy. However, I've tried my best to meet my spouse's needs, take care of my children, and dedicate time to work. If you want to know how I did it, you just have to keep reading. As a first-time dad, I made many mistakes. I've been through difficult times and struggled to maintain a healthy and positive relationship with my wife. At the same time, I've been constantly worried I was about to ruin my children's lives. After years of experience, expertise, and practice, I've decided to gather all the information I acquired and put it in a book—*this* book.

Here, you'll find a holistic approach to fatherhood that helps you tackle issues in all aspects of your life. In the first chapter, you'll discover how the role of the father has changed over the centuries, how to foster a positive home environment and support your partner, and how to navigate pregnancy together. In Chapter 2, you'll learn to develop a positive and growth mindset to promote your child's development. In Chapter 3, you'll find out how to understand your baby's emotions and needs and how to cultivate a deep connection through practical techniques. Chapter 4 will discuss how to find a balance between work and family by managing time and setting boundaries. Chapter 5 will dive deep into the topic of the changing relationship with your partner and will show you how to improve communication and understand their emotional and physical changes.

In Chapter 6, you'll learn to address the most common challenges linked with fatherhood, such as sleep deprivation and typical fears and anxieties. Chapter 7 will teach you how to create a long-lasting bond with your child from the first day of their life. In Chapter 8, you'll discover the importance of your presence and engagement and how to develop both in your relationship with your little one. Finally, Chapter 9 will discuss some insights about the future, like financial planning and your child's transition from infancy to adolescence. At the end of each chapter, you'll also find an interactive element to put into practice the newly acquired information. After finishing reading this book and applying the methods and techniques discussed, you'll be better prepared for the journey of fatherhood. You'll develop a deeper emotional connection with both your significant other and child, understand the changing dynamics of your relationship, and effectively balance work and family life. Additionally, you'll be more culturally aware, equipped to face common challenges, and focused on building a strong foundation for the future. You'll not only become an effective father, but you'll also nurture a wholesome family environment.

Before reading this book and practicing the activities, you must keep in mind a few essential concepts. First, there's no perfect dad. All fathers make mistakes even if they have the best intentions and put all their effort into raising their children. Even if you prepare and look for as much information as you can in books or the internet, and ask for other fathers' help, you'll never be fully ready. Being a father is an art that can only be learned through trial and error. Obviously, you can prepare yourself, but you'll surely face obstacles and events you didn't expect and couldn't predict in any way. Second, you might find yourself on an emotional roller-coaster, especially during the first few months after birth. You might love your baby and also find them irritating from time to time. You might have negative thoughts about fatherhood and raising children because your relationship with your partner has drastically changed. You might be distant one day and draw closer another. Finally, there's no instruction manual to raise your baby properly. Each child is unique, so they all grow at different rates and develop different skills. What you must always remember as you help your child grow is to be flexible and adaptable and keep learning. This book will give you all the tools you need, but it will be your responsibility to adjust them according to your specific situation.

1

The Landscape of Fatherhood

The heart of a father is the masterpiece of nature.

Antoine François Prévost d'Exiles

In this chapter, we'll take a look at the big picture. We'll discover how fatherhood evolved throughout the centuries, from ancient practices and roles to modern changes. Next, we'll learn how to be supportive during pregnancy and promote open communication. We'll also learn the importance of attending prenatal classes together and understanding the physical and emotional changes in our partners. Then, we'll discover how to foster a positive home environment and embrace cultural diversity by becoming aware of how different cultures perceive fatherhood. Finally, we'll learn to create our unique family culture, also considering community resources and cultural mentors' help to apply culturally responsive parenting practices. By the end of the chapter, you'll have a complete understanding of fatherhood and how it changes through time and culture.

Historical Perspectives of Fatherhood

What did it mean to be a father two or three centuries ago (*The Changing Role of the Modern Day Father*, 2009)? It meant being the family breadwinner and conveying moral values and religious education to their children. The word "breadwinner" is used to define a type of dynamic where men make all the decisions and provide for the family. In such families, women usually don't work and are expected to take care of household duties and children. Conversely, men must work and don't have to be present to foster a positive home environment. They must also teach their children social etiquette and how to be disciplined and respect the rules. This type of family is considered traditional, as it was very common before the advent of urbanization and industrialization when people moved from the countryside to the modern cities and worked in factories. However, as society changed, so did the role of fathers and mothers. In general, widowed or unmarried women increased, and fathers were even more detached from family duties due to the long working hours and strenuous jobs (*The Changing Role of the Modern Day Father*, 2009).

An important new change in the role of fatherhood occurred when World War II ended, and Western societies kept developing financially and economically (*The Changing Role of the*

Modern Day Father, 2009). The traditional breadwinner family model began to crumble as women entered the workforce of the most developed Western economies and began earning their own salaries. Therefore, men weren't expected to be the sole providers for the family anymore, and women weren't expected to only stay home and take care of children. Since the end of the 1940s, the father's role has kept changing and adapting to new needs and situations. Divorce and remarriage have kept increasing, childbirth outside of marriage has become more frequent, and fertility has declined. The breadwinner family has gradually become less prominent, and fathers have become more interested in taking care of their children and helping. In the last 20 to 30 years, research has begun to focus on fathers' involvement in children's development and household duties (*The Changing Role of the Modern Day Father*, 2009). Now, most of them actively participate in parenting their children. It's also more common to see single fathers or fathers who prefer working from home or taking parental leave to spend more time with their families. Today, it's easy to spot a father in a park playing with their children or pushing a stroller.

In Western societies, the father's role has continued to change over the centuries. However, in some places, men still have to face the same challenges their ancestors did (McKay & McKay, 2010). Some tribes still organize men's rites of passage from childhood or adolescence to manhood or masculinity. Interestingly, the Sambia tribe of Papua New Guinea is characterized by different stages of manhood. After the steps of childhood and puberty, a man has the full rights of masculinity only after becoming a father, thus making fatherhood the most crucial moment in men's lives (McKay & McKay, 2010).

The Evolving Role of Modern Dads

Let's see in detail how the role of fathers has changed in the last decades. At the end of World War II, fathers became aware of two different parental functions: traditional and conceptual (Check, 2019). The traditional function includes teaching children how to behave correctly and respect rules, while the conceptual function implies teaching children how to develop self-esteem and self-reliance and how to properly interact with others. Fathers began to realize the conceptual function was just as important as the traditional one, so they aimed at being happy and positive people for the sake of their children's physical and mental health. In the meantime, the concept of gender equality began to spread among the various countries of the Western world. Women asked for the same rights and privileges as men. They wanted to work the same amount of time, get paid the same salary, and achieve the same social benefits. They also wanted more freedom of choice about their household duties. In the last few decades, gender equality has become much more than just a concept—it's a reality (Check, 2019).

There are fewer and fewer differences between women and men. Fathers spend more time at home, taking care of the house and children more than they used to. They're more involved in their children's hobbies, activities, and duties, and help with grocery shopping, laundry, and other chores. Here's a practical example of how fatherhood has rapidly changed: Just think about how the role of fathers in delivery rooms has become more significant (Prichep, 2017). Until the beginning of the 20th century, most women gave birth in their homes and were surrounded by other women in their families and groups of friends. Therefore, fathers were left behind. Beginning in the 1930s, more and more women gave birth to their children in hospitals but felt lonelier because they weren't surrounded by their loved ones. At the same time, fathers became increasingly unhappy about being left in waiting rooms and not being able to be present and supportive during the birth of their child. It took some time, but by the end of the 1960s, fathers were allowed to enter the delivery rooms during labor in Western societies. By the end of the 1980s, they could also attend the moment of their child's birth (Prichep, 2017). If you think about it, so much progress has been made in allowing fathers to actively engage and support their partners. Now, we can say mothers and fathers are a team that collaborates in close contact.

Navigating Pregnancy Together: Understanding and Supporting Your Partner During Pregnancy

During pregnancy, most of the attention revolves around the mother who gives birth to the child. They undergo important physical changes that must be kept under constant observation to protect the child's health. Therefore, fathers might feel like their support and involvement are not needed or necessary. However, that couldn't be further from the truth. Much of research suggests that the father's involvement is essential to ensure the child's and mother's safety (*New Dads and Partners:*

How Your Involvement Matters, 2023). For example, mothers are more likely to receive appropriate medical care when fathers are present and are more likely to quit smoking if their partners support them. Moreover, rates of premature birth and infant mortality decrease when the father is involved during pregnancy. Fathers also play an important role during children's development (*Fathers: Powerful Allies for Maternal and Child Health*, n.d.). They support the advancement of social and emotional skills and help their children understand how the world works. Without them, children would lack a significant source of information and emotional support. As a father, you shouldn't consider yourself a mere supportive addition but realize that your actions significantly impact on your child's lifelong health. Your partner wouldn't be able to effectively handle pregnancy without you, and your child will feel the effect of your absence (*Fathers: Powerful Allies for Maternal and Child Health*, n.d.).

The Importance of Communication and Emotional Support

During pregnancy and the days after childbirth, communication and emotional support can make a difference in how your significant other faces such an intense moment. For example, they might experience frequent mood swings or postnatal "blues" that make them feel bad. This means they will need all your support to overcome such a hard time. How can you make sure you provide all the support your partner needs? You can follow some easy tips.

First, you must educate yourself, especially during pregnancy when you still have the time. The more knowledge you acquire about pregnancy, the more powerful and confident you will feel. As mentioned in the introduction, it doesn't automatically mean you'll be able to face all obstacles, as some can't be predicted. However, you can provide your partner with much practical support. Read pregnancy books, attend childbirth classes, and talk to other parents who can advise you. The more information you manage to gather, the more you'll be prepared. Just make sure not to overload yourself with too much information. You might find all sorts of facts, evidence, and advice out there, so try to filter everything. You can focus on information that aligns with your traditions, values, and culture. But keep in mind there's no cookie-cutter or one-size-fits-all approach to parenting. Just look for information and focus on what you consider more relevant and valuable for you.

You can also show your partner what you learn and discuss it together to make decisions as a couple. Another way of offering emotional support and improving communication is to attend as many medical appointments and duties linked with pregnancy as you can. If you keep pace with all the emotional and physical changes that are happening and all the things that happen and will occur shortly, you're more likely to understand them. Being very supportive at home might not be enough to foster effective communication; don't be scared to learn from experts.

To effectively communicate, you must keep an open mind and be willing to listen. Pregnancy might not only provoke negative emotions but also bring up painful memories, increase fears and anxieties, and make your loved ones doubt themselves. They might be afraid they won't be able to care for their child. In such cases, they need someone who can calmly listen to them and accept their emotions. They must feel like they can tell you whatever crosses their minds without feeling guilty or ashamed. If you know how you can emotionally support them, you're more likely to make them feel good. If not, there's nothing to worry about, as it's impossible to always know what they need and want—especially during pregnancy when their mood switches often. To be supportive and develop open communication, ask what you can do for them. Sometimes, we forget about the little deeds that make others happy. Luckily, we can ask them to ensure we are doing the right thing.

Attending Prenatal Classes and Medical Appointments Together

Prenatal care is fundamental to ensure the mother and the child are healthy during and after childbirth. Prenatal care includes classes that help your partner prepare to give birth to a child and medical appointments. As mentioned above, your presence is paramount to improving their mood and ensuring your child is safe and healthy. Therefore, you must accompany them to the visits and classes to know and understand what will happen in the following weeks and months. In fact, prenatal classes are essential in teaching you everything you need to know about birth, breastfeeding, pregnancy, and how to transition from a family of two to parenthood. Such classes might give you valuable insights and spark questions you wouldn't have considered of yourself. Moreover, they help you communicate your choices to your doctor and express your feelings and thoughts to your partner. They're also a good way of meeting other soon-to-be parents in the same situation. You can exchange information with them, express your concerns, and find support. For all the above reasons, you shouldn't underestimate the usefulness of prenatal classes.

But how do prenatal classes work in practice? You can choose among different types, as they usually analyze a specific topic, such as breastfeeding or labor. If you look on the internet, you can find an infinite number of classes from which you can choose. Before signing up for classes, find as much information as possible about them. In fact, they might follow different methods or review labor techniques. Make sure you choose the class that best suits your needs and might appeal to you more. Moreover, you must decide as soon as possible because prenatal classes usually fill up quickly. You might want to start them months before the due date. Now, you might wonder what will actually happen during classes. First, your partner will officially choose you as a labor coach, which is the person who will assist them during labor. Then, an instructor will teach you how to handle labor together. They will show you practices concerning various stages of labor and ways to control pain and stay relaxed to ensure the delivery proceeds smoothly. You'll practice such strategies until classes finish and your partner is ready to give birth.

Understanding the Physical Changes and Emotional Needs of Your Partner

In addition to emotionally and practically supporting your loved one, you must also understand the most significant changes they undergo during pregnancy. The more you know about their needs, the better they'll feel and the healthier your baby will be. Knowing the essential physical and emotional changes, you can also effectively help them.

The most influential hormones during pregnancy are estrogen and progesterone. Did you know that women produce more estrogen while they're pregnant than in the rest of their lives (*What Bodily Changes Can You Expect During Pregnancy*, 2012)? That's because estrogen is paramount in the proper development of the fetus. Thanks to it, the baby receives all the nutrients it needs and forms blood vessels. Estrogen is also responsible for the common nausea associated with the first trimester of pregnancy. In fact, it's because estrogen levels increase so rapidly that women feel nauseous. At the same time, progesterone causes a loosening of ligaments and joints, thus raising the risk of sprains and strains. Pregnant women also gain weight and retain more fluids and their faces and limbs might swell. As you might guess, pregnancy increases the workload on a woman's body, so they should be careful with exercise and physical activity (*What Bodily Changes Can You Expect During Pregnancy*, 2012).

Physical changes are also accompanied by sensory changes that drastically modify the perception of the world around them. For example, pregnant women are likely to experience increased nearsightedness and blurriness and might feel less comfortable putting contact lenses on (*What Bodily Changes Can You Expect During Pregnancy*, 2012). Research is still trying to understand how pregnancy affects women's vision, but it has found clear results about the influence of pregnancy on taste. In general, pregnant women prefer saltier and sweeter foods, and their taste preferences might vary over the months. Most of them also report an increased sense of smell that makes them identify more odors and various intensities, but no conclusive evidence has confirmed this (*What Bodily Changes Can You Expect During Pregnancy*, 2012).

Creating a Supportive Environment at Home

When your baby finally enters this world, they'll significantly change your lifestyle and habits. For this reason, you must start caring for yourself and your partner before childbirth. Preparing yourself will help you foster a positive and stress-free home environment and help you both face such a delicate time in your lives.

To create a supportive home environment, you must take care of yourself first. You must maintain a healthy weight to avoid stress, obesity, or other mental and physical conditions that might hinder your success as a father (*25 Things to Do When Preparing for Fatherhood*, 2022). Therefore, you must develop a well-balanced diet and participate in regular exercise. You must ensure you drink enough water daily and eat fruit and vegetables. Moreover, you must consider physical activity you could easily practice after childbirth. Keep in mind you'll spend most of your energy and time taking care of your child, so you'll have less time for yourself. That's why you must think of ways to eat healthy and keep fit without having to go to the gym or spend hours working out. To feel less stressed and avoid feeling over-whelmed after your child's arrival, you must also create a sleep schedule or routine with your significant other. You'll realize sleep is a precious commodity, so plan your sleep schedule together and regularly adjust it. In general, you must find ways to manage your mental health. Check in with your loved one and your emotions from time to time, openly communicate how you feel, and do activities you enjoy. You must dedicate time to yourself and encourage them to do the same.

You must also take care of some domestic tasks that will facili-tate your life after childbirth. For example, you can start cooking and freezing meals in advance. Take some time to decide what you both want to eat and store some meals in the freezer. This way, you'll get used to having some precooked tasty meals ready to eat when you're in a rush or don't feel like cooking. To prepare yourself for your child's arrival, you can also start baby-proofing your home. You'll quickly realize how fast they grow and learn to move around by themselves, so to avoid doing all the work when you don't have a lot of time and energy, you can baby-proof your house in advance.

You can find everything you need at a baby store. You'll find a lot of items, but they're not all useful and essential. What you should focus on is a crib, diaper pail, car seat, changing table, and baby bathtub. Finally, a clean and healthy environment is essential for your little one; thus, you should check your living space is thoroughly clean and rearrange spaces if necessary.

Make room for all the furniture and items you'll need to take care of your baby and get rid of all the items that might be dangerous for them or that you don't need any more by donating them or putting them in your garage or somewhere safe.

Embracing Cultural Diversity: Adapting Fatherhood Techniques Across Different Cultures

Recognizing and Respecting the Rich Tapestry of Cultural Traditions and Practices in Parenting

Now, let's look more in detail at what it means to be a father. Interestingly, there's no right answer that clearly explains what fatherhood entails. In fact, it implies different elements according to the sociocultural context and individual background. If you've ever discussed fatherhood with your friends, you might have noticed they attach various meanings to it. And that's normal, as we've all been raised differently in different environments. Your friends and you have probably been raised in the same area, so imagine how many changes you could notice in diverse cultures worldwide.

For example, fatherhood in Brazil is influenced by the cultural heritage of slavery and colonialism when fathers were absent, social classes were deeply divided, and patriarchy was the norm (Shwalb & Shwalb, 2014). Still today, mothers take care of their children more than fathers, who only teach them essential skills to be able to work and have proper etiquette. This type of fatherhood is not so different from the breadwinner model we discussed at the beginning of the chapter. Moreover, Brazil is such a big country that fatherhood is perceived differently according to the geographical area. In some regions, fathers are actively involved and engaged in their role and help during pregnancy and after childbirth. Another example of cultural differences is in Bangladesh, where Bengalis are the predominant ethnic group. In this case, fathers are moderately involved in their role. They care for their sons and daughters equally but do it less than mothers. In fact, women are still the primary caregivers in the family. But the above are just two examples of how fatherhood changes throughout cultures. Did you know that Russian fathers are considered "secondary parents," superfluous, and even irresponsible? They're perceived so negatively that they tend to maintain a detached behavior with their children (Shwalb & Shwalb, 2014).

Adapting Your Approach to Fatherhood to Honor Cultural Norms, Values, and Expectations

How can you be a good father? You must learn to adapt your values to the cultural norms of the society you'll raise your child in, which might not be easy. Paternal investment can vary a lot from family to family, also depending on how fathers have been raised by their parents and their personal past experiences (Roopnarine & Yildirim, 2016). Moreover, they might live together with their children or live elsewhere due to duties like their job. At the same time, they might be involved and engaged or not. Fathers who live with their children might be emotionally detached, while those who live far away might find new and unique ways to feel close to their children and maintain a connection. Paternal involvement also depends on the economic status, how men are perceived in their country, and residential patterns. If fathers live in a country where masculinity is given value, they might choose to be strict and detached from their children. Conversely, they might create a deep connection in countries where men and women are considered equal, and their duties are distributed. In rare cases, some societies expect fathers to be even more involved than mothers (Roopnarine & Yildirim, 2016).

Moreover, there's no single way to support your child's development. In fact, research has found that fathers can have a positive impact on their children's development by engaging in a vast array of behaviors. For example, fathers can promote a positive home environment by fostering a relationship based on quality. They might not spend a lot of time with their children, but they dedicate all of themselves when they can. They might nurture family solidarity by organizing activities together. They might also prefer being emotionally rather than physically present with their children. However, research agrees that warmth and sensitivity are the two elements that achieve the best results in a child's development in all countries (Roopnarine & Yildirim, 2016). Therefore, an emotionally present father who expresses love and affection is likelier to create a strong relationship with their children.

Collaborating With Your Partner to Blend Traditions and Create a Unique Family Culture

Take a few seconds to reflect on your past experiences and the sociocultural norms you're attached to. How were you raised? Where do you come from? Do your parents come from a culture different from the one you're actually living in? Then, discuss the same topics with your partner and ask them about the traditions and culture they feel closer to. You both might come from different backgrounds. For example, you might come from South America and speak Spanish, while your partner might be born and raised in the US. This means you have different traditions and are used to different sociocultural norms. There's nothing to worry about or be ashamed of, as we're all different in some way—even a person from Nevada and one from California. However, you must find the perfect balance to blend your traditions together and support your child's proper development.

Let's take the above example. If you come from South America and speak Spanish, you might decide to speak your language with your children and teach them some ancient traditions linked with your culture. If your partner is North American, they might want to speak American English and teach them about the traditions of their home state. You can integrate both cultures to help your child speak two languages, become bilingual, and combine different traditions. Even if you both come from the same country or state, you can still blend your cultures. You might have lived for years in Europe or other countries worldwide and have assimilated part of their cultures, as your significant other might have done, too. You can discuss your past together and decide which culture suits both of you the best. Remember to always consider the cultural norms of your area and try to find a compromise between the two so that your child doesn't feel like they're entirely different from their peers.

Seeking Community Resources or Cultural Mentors to Guide Your Understanding and Application of Culturally Responsive Parenting Practices

During pregnancy, you might feel lonely, as most of the attention is centered on the mother and your baby, not you. You might feel abandoned and look for support. Alternatively, you might happily face pregnancy but look for help to know what's best to do. In both cases, you can turn to your local community or online. You can look for initiatives organized by local authorities or organizations to help fathers in particular, or families in general, to handle pregnancy and the baby's arrival. You can also meet other fathers and discuss fatherhood together. Previously in this chapter, we discussed the importance of being prepared for your child's arrival and buying what you need. Well, you can take advantage of those situations to meet other fathers and have a chat with them. You might find you have more things in common than you think and that they're willing to help you. In general, hanging out in the same places parents go will help you find people who understand and can help.

If you're not comfortable finding help face-to-face, you can do it online. If you look online, you'll find plenty of websites, forums, and communities where fathers discuss their lives, give advice, and support other fathers. You can find online groups for families, couples, mothers and fathers, or only fathers. If you're comfortable with social media, you can discover influencers on Instagram or TikTok that show you what a dad's life looks like, including the difficulties and highlights. They usually offer practical tips and advice on how to prepare to become a dad and what to do in the first few weeks and months after childbirth. Just go out there and discover new resources to help you raise your child and blend your traditions with the sociocultural norms you live in.

Interactive Element

Let's reflect on all the information we acquired throughout the chapter. Ask yourself the following thought-provoking questions or discuss them with your loved ones. You can also use them in group discussions if you're part of a book club or study group. If you want, you can write down the answers to the following questions in a journal to record and look at them after some time, such as after childbirth or when your baby is a few months old.

Historical Perspective and Modern Evolution

- How do you think the role of fathers has changed from your grandfather's generation to yours?

- In what ways do you believe society's expectations of fathers have evolved in the last few decades?

Navigating Pregnancy Together

- How has your perception of pregnancy changed since learning about your partner's experience?
- If you've ever felt left out or secondary during the pregnancy process, how did you cope and find your own unique role?

Communication and Emotional Support

- Can you recall a situation where you felt out of depth in supporting your partner? How did you handle it, and what did you learn?
- In which ways do you feel you could improve your communication skills during the pregnancy phase?

Attending Prenatal Classes and Medical Appointments

- How did attending prenatal classes or medical appointments change your understanding of pregnancy?
- Describe a memorable moment during a prenatal class or appointment that deepened your bond with your partner.

Understanding Physical and Emotional Changes

- Were there any physical or emotional changes in your significant other that took you by surprise? How did you adapt?
- How did you ensure you were present and supportive during moments of heightened emotional vulnerability?

In this chapter, we thoroughly discussed how the role of fathers changes throughout time and place. We discovered that most fathers were supposed to work and provide for the family while mothers cared for the children. Recently, fathers have become increasingly involved and support mothers in raising their children. To truly help, we must learn how pregnancy works and stay emotionally close. We must become aware of the main physical and emotional changes they undergo during pregnancy and attend prenatal classes and medical appointments to show we care and want to be present. Finally, we looked at how different cultures perceive fatherhood and how our personal traditions and cultural norms can influence the way we raise our children. To retain all the information, we acquired and reflect on ourselves, we can do the above activity. Now that we know everything about the role of fathers, we can move on to Chapter 2 to find out what we can do in our daily lives to support our loved ones and our children's development. In the next chapter, we'll discover how cultivating the right mindset can positively change our perspective on fatherhood.

2

Cultivating the Right Mindset

I magine driving through a tunnel with no end in sight—sounds like a nightmare, right? Now, imagine there's a sign that says, "Ends in 500 feet," and instantly, your perspective changes. Fatherhood is that tunnel, and your mindset is that sign. How many times have you told yourself you can't do it because you're afraid you won't be a good father or won't be able to support your partner properly? Stop for a few seconds and reflect on all your doubts: Do they come from inside you, or are they just stereotypes? Was your father emotionally distant and influenced the way you perceive paternal figures? If so, you're no different from other fathers. Since you were little, you were probably surrounded by common beliefs about being a father that still impacts your perception. In this chapter, you'll learn to let go of them to embrace a positive and growth mindset that will accompany you throughout your fatherhood journey.

The Power of Positive Thinking in Fatherhood

In life, you'll always have to face challenges. As a father, you might have to struggle with various difficulties along the path of helping your child grow. There could be days you won't be able to appreciate all the good things you have, and you feel like you're doomed. Some days, you might love your child and have fun with your family. Others, you might regret your choice of having a baby. You might feel like you're not suited to be a good father and you don't know how to raise your child. Bright days are easy to face because you feel good, while dark days might be challenging. For this reason, you must find yourself a useful ally: Positive thinking.

Positive thinking is the ability to focus on the good things that happen to you. Even during the darkest hours or days, you know how to focus on the positive aspects of your life, such as how much you love your partner and how much they love you back, all the progress your baby makes every day, and all the support you receive from other people. If you regularly practice positive thinking, you can increase your happiness and overall well-being (*Positive Thinking*, 2022). In fact, positive thinking makes you feel less sad and helps you stop worrying about all the negative things that happen to you.

The real secret behind practicing positive thinking is that you must believe in it and get used to thinking positively every day. The American novelist Henry James said, "Be not afraid of life. Believe that life is worth living, and your belief will help create the fact" (Dungy, 2015). In other words, believing in all the opportunities and good things that happen to you allows you to look at the bright side and notice more opportunities and good things. Our minds are powerful instruments that can shape how we perceive the world. If you keep thinking you'll never make it and you'll ruin your relationship with your significant other, you're more likely to make it happen. If you believe in your skills and ability to face obstacles, you can overcome them. Moreover, practicing positive thinking in front of and with your child can encourage them to do the same. If they always see you sad, unsatisfied, stressed, and frustrated, they might start feeling the same feelings and, thus, develop a negative mindset that makes them see the world as a dark place. Conversely, seeing you happy and positive about the future can make them hopeful and optimistic.

The more you practice positive thinking, the easier it becomes over time. If you think about it, the same is true in the opposite scenario. If you always focus on the negative aspects of your life, you're more likely to notice them even more. How can you practice positive thinking to improve your and your baby's life? You just need to become aware of all the good things and how you've made them happen. Keep in mind that every effect has its cause. If your loved one buys you a nice gift, might it be because you did something nice for them and they want to thank you? If your baby smiles at you, is it because you smiled at them first? You have the power to feel happier and help your child develop positive thinking by focusing on good deeds. Try to reflect on one positive event every day and ask yourself how you made it happen. Once you get used to it, you'll notice more and more positive things every day.

Challenges to Mindset and Overcoming Limiting Beliefs

To practice positive thinking, you mustn't only focus on the positive aspects of your life, but you must also fight against obstacles. As a father, what hinders your success are popular stereotypes that might make you believe you're not able to raise your child properly. Such stereotypes can influence your perception of fatherhood so much that you end up excluding yourself from taking care of your baby and helping out. In other words, stereotypes might make you look at the dark side and increase pessimistic thinking, making you engage in negative behaviors that only worsen the situation.

Do you know what the most common stereotypes about fatherhood are? Two of them include considering the father the sole breadwinner and the authority figure of the family. In the previous chapter, we discussed how fathers were perceived as needing to provide for their families and educate their children to respect rules. For centuries, those were the main roles fathers played at home. However, dads don't have to be like that anymore. In fact, many of them now support their partners' career aspirations and collaborate with them. They prefer a democratic decision-making process in which they consider their children's needs and wants and not only force them to follow the rules. Over the decades, fathers have also been depicted as tough guys, absent, and incompetent. Society has always taught men that they must be tough and never show emotions in order to appeal to women. More recently, men have understood the importance of vulnerability and how expressing emotions deepen their connection with others.

Modern fathers also want to be actively engaged in all the activities their children practice and want to participate in their lives. Consequently, they've also shown they're not as incompetent as society might make them believe. They're able to change diapers, manage household chores, and prepare meals, just like their partners.

Another popular stereotype is that fathers can't be as nurturing as mothers. However, many dads nowadays demonstrate that they're perfectly capable of caring for their children, even without someone else's help. Until recently, fathers also felt the need to reproduce the traditional gender roles of fathers and mothers. Therefore, they didn't feel comfortable doing tasks that were considered exclusively for women, like cooking or cleaning the house. More recently, dads have become unafraid of fighting gender roles and showing they also enjoy doing activities generally associated with women. Other two common stereotypes that developed during the previous century concern fathers being only interested in work and sports. Fathers were used to working many hours to provide for their families and put their jobs before anything else—even their mental and physical health. Nowadays, fathers value the concept of work-life balance and don't consider their work as important as past paternal figures did. Moreover, men can have diverse interests beyond sports. Therefore, they can bond with their children in other ways rather than by practicing athletic activities together. Obviously, practicing sports and bonding by watching football on the TV isn't bad per se. However, it's not the only way in which fathers and children can create a deep connection.

The word "maternal" refers to everything related to being a mother, while the word "paternal" concerns all aspects of fatherhood (Adams, 2022). Due to this gendered difference in terminology, we believe mothers have intrinsic maternal instincts while fathers don't. The correct terminology should be "parental," as raising children doesn't only involve maternal or paternal abilities but concerns both parents at the same level. In fact, research has found that the ability to raise a child properly is connected with the parent's sense of competence in their parenting role (Adams, 2022). This means that a competent parent is more likely to raise a happy and satisfied child. If you think about it, feeling competent is an aspect of practicing positive thinking. Therefore, mothers can be as good or bad at parenting as fathers can. If you want, you can be "maternal" and effectively nurture your baby.

Embracing Change and Growth in the Fatherhood Journey

Do you fear stepping out of your comfort zone? Having a child is not so different from trying a new and scary activity on your own. Becoming a father involves many challenges that might make you reconsider your thoughts and feel discouraged. Even embracing positive thinking might mean leaving your comfort zone and might make you feel awkward or nervous. Therefore, you might fall into the trap of your old habits and routines and decide you're doing better, just like now. Alternatively, you might believe leaving your comfort zone means forcing a change on yourself. In both cases, you have a negative perception of change and see it as something others or even life imposes on you, and there's nothing you can do about it.

Well, you're not entirely wrong. Change is inevitable—no matter if you want it or not. Moreover, change will never be easy, as it will always cause you some pain. Getting rid of old habits and adapting to new situations requires time, energy, and effort. Therefore, you might prefer continuing to do the same things, even if they're not particularly helpful or advantageous. However, you can't say change is forced on you, as you can do something about it: You can take the opportunity to grow.

We tend to consider growth and change as synonyms, but they're slightly different. In fact, growing entails improving your life, thus meaning you have power over it. Conversely, change is an external factor that influences your life positively or negatively. You might consider raising a child as a change because you feel like it just happened to you, and you can't do anything about it. However, fatherhood can be a way of growing. You don't have to passively endure change, but transform it into an opportunity to improve and become a better person. Every time you tell yourself something like, *That's who I am, and I can't change*, reflect on your ability to take action to grow as an individual. Do you really have no power over who you are? You'll always change and be able to grow.

But how can you embrace change and grow? First of all, you must accept everything that happens to you. You must never fight events, emotions, and thoughts. If you don't accept change, you're more likely to face it with a negative attitude, thus increasing your probability of failing. Remember, change is inevitable, so you'd better face it with the right attitude— positive thinking. If you think positively, you see everything has a meaning and can be seen as an opportunity to improve. Therefore, you see the glass half full and consider all the benefits change can have in your life.

In addition to raising your child, another change might involve your romantic relationship. You might feel like they no longer have time for you and only focus on the newborn baby. In this case, too, you must embrace change as an opportunity to grow and improve your relationship. For example, you can consider boosting your communication skills and discussing together a time when you're both available and willing to freely express your thoughts and emotions.

Techniques for Cultivating Resilience and Adaptability

To develop a positive and growth mindset, you must also cultivate resilience, which is the ability to go through significant life events without feeling overwhelmed and crushed. If you're resilient, you can adequately face challenges and grow as an individual. In fact, being resilient doesn't mean overcoming obstacles and starting again. If you go through stressful events, you'll never be the same person again. You'll create a new version of yourself, change your priorities, or improve your relationships. Being resilient involves accepting change and using positive thinking to become a better person. When your baby finally arrives, and you officially become a father, you'll never be the same. However, you can grow by prioritizing your baby over your job and friends, seeing yourself as a father more than a partner or son, becoming aware of abilities you didn't think you had, and building stronger relationships with others.

As you can see, becoming a father can have many advantages and can improve your life.

If you're not resilient enough, you might believe you'll never be able to properly raise your child, or you might face obstacles with a negative attitude. You might also develop anxiety or depression and fear of making mistakes and ruining your child's future. If you lack resilience and want to improve, you can learn to adapt to change. In general, you must practice all the activities that promote your mental health and personal well-being. You can also follow some easy tips.

As you learned in the previous section, you must accept and embrace change. Choose to adapt to it instead of passively enduring it and become aware that it's part of your daily life. You might have pursued a personal goal for years and then realized you could never achieve it. If that happens, just accept change and move on with your life. You can find a new goal or focus on the ones you're still pursuing. As for your goals, you must make them attainable and realistic. Only if you succeed at what you do can you develop resilience. Therefore, you must ensure you have the right skills to successfully achieve your goals. Take small steps and divide your goals into parts so you don't have to accomplish many complex tasks simultaneously. The more you succeed, the more you feel self-confident and aware that you can face all sorts of obstacles.

To become more resilient, you must see difficulties and crises as opportunities, not insurmountable. In other words, you must always have a positive mindset and see the good things that happen to you and all the goals you manage to achieve.

Moreover, you must always keep the big picture in mind and consider the broader context. As a father, you might make many mistakes over the years, and you won't always understand what your baby needs, especially when they're very little. Maintain your perspective and pursue the goal of becoming a good father. Accept you might make some mistakes, but be aware of all your small successes and steps you make daily to feel closer to your baby. Finally, becoming resilient means asking for help. You mustn't face obstacles alone and can share your doubts and fears with your partner and friends. Let your loved ones help you and do something for you.

Interactive Element

Now, let's put into practice what you've learned in this chapter. Use the following journal prompts to write your own journal and as inspiration to reflect on the events that happen in your life. Think about challenging moments you faced during the day or week and how you overcame them. Consider your feelings, thoughts, and actions to understand if you're successfully practicing positive thinking and taking action to improve your life. You can jot down your thoughts and emotions or reflect on the following sentences.

- What does being a father mean to you?
- What are your biggest fears, and how do you plan to overcome them?
- Is there something your father taught you that you would like to teach your child?
- What do you want to do differently from your father?

- What are some of the values and beliefs you want to pass on to your child?
- Describe one of the funniest and most stressful moments you had since you knew you would become a father.
- What do you appreciate the most in your partner and in the way they're handling pregnancy?
- Have you noticed some changes in your romantic relationship lately? If so, try to describe them.
- Is there a specific activity you would like to do with your child?
- Do you consider yourself optimistic? Why?
- Is there something that always puts you in a good mood?
- How does your significant other manage to lift your spirit? What do you do to cheer them up?
- What could you do to develop a more positive mindset?
- Each day, write down something you're thankful for.
- From time to time, remind yourself that it's human to make mistakes.
- What can you do today to make someone else's day better?
- What are some qualities you value in yourself and others?
- What negative thing could you easily eliminate from your life?
- Write about a time you used positive thinking to reframe a negative situation.

- What healthy habits do you wish to maintain after your child's birth? What habits would you like to get rid of? How would you eliminate them?

The above sentences are just examples to show you the questions you can ask yourself or things you can reflect on. Don't hesitate to expand on them to go a little deeper.

In this chapter, we discussed the importance of positive thinking and how we can develop a growth and positive mindset. Seeing things from the right perspective can help us achieve our goals and become good fathers. It also helps us fight common stereotypes that set us back from success. We must always believe in our skills and regularly practice positive thinking to make it a natural daily activity. We must also learn to perceive fatherhood as a positive change and an opportunity to grow and become resilient by caring for our overall well-being and mental health. Finally, we discovered an easy activity we can do every day to become aware of our thoughts, emotions, and actions and practice positive thinking. In the next chapter, we'll dive deep into the topic of emotions and how you can create a deep and long-lasting emotional bond with your baby.

3

The Emotional Bond

The first three years of your child's life will be paramount for their development (Maltese, 2015). Your baby will grow emotionally and physically faster during the first three years than the rest of their life. When your baby is 3, they'll have developed 85% of their brain (Maltese, 2015). This means that your involvement in the first years of their life is essential to foster positive development, especially concerning emotional regulation. If you know your baby needs supportive and loving relationships, you're more likely to help them learn to love and be loved. In other words, your child understands that they matter and that their parents are fundamental to survival. If you effectively respond to your baby's needs, you help them recognize and understand emotions. Suppose you want to nurture a positive relationship with your child. In that case, you must understand their emotional needs, foster a deep connection from the moment they arrive in your life, and appropriately interact with them through touch, talk, and play.

That's precisely what you'll learn in this chapter. In the last section, you'll also find a practical activity to keep track of your baby's progress.

Understanding Your Child's Emotional Needs

As a father, you might value your baby's intellectual and physical development. Obviously, improving cognitive function and being physically strong are both essential elements in your child's life. However, emotional and social development is just as crucial. If your baby feels safe and happy, they will be more likely to enjoy learning new things and be emotionally stable as an adult (McIlroy, 2019). Why is developing emotional skills so essential for your child? Well, if they know how to handle their emotions properly, they're more likely to be emotionally healthy as an adult. Therefore, they'll feel more satisfied, happier, and less stressed. They'll also be able to develop stronger and deeper relationships with their friends and other people they'll meet in their lives, and they'll feel more self-confident. Moreover, they'll know how to make effective decisions for themselves, and they won't easily give up to peer pressure.

The earlier you start taking care of your baby's emotional and social development, the more likely they'll become happy and confident adults. To foster their emotional development, you must first understand their basic emotional needs. Your child needs to feel secure and safe at home. If you show them your love and foster a safe home environment, they'll probably feel confident enough to explore new places by themselves, thus growing and learning. Your child needs to try new activities as much as they need a routine. Therefore, you must make sure you let them do the same things often. Children feel more comfortable and safer when their days are predictable, and they know what will happen next. Moreover, helping your child follow a routine at home promotes a smooth adjustment to school routines. Your baby also needs discipline and consistency to understand the difference between healthy and acceptable behaviors and unhealthy and inappropriate ones. Your child needs approval and acceptance to feel safe and appreciated. This means you must accept them as they are and don't try to force changes on them. They need to understand you love them unconditionally, and they're worthy of love.

How can you support your child's emotional development? The tip that's always valid is to be a good example. Your child will learn a lot from you, and they'll probably try to repeat your actions. If they see you often lying, they might learn to do the same with their friends and loved ones. If you show them your love and care for others, they'll be more likely to understand how to show love to others effectively. To support their emotional development, you must give space to emotions. Learn to express how you feel and often discuss emotions with your child. Teach them the importance of being grateful and clearly saying "Thank you," "I'm sorry," and "Please." Explain the reasons behind your emotions to help them understand what triggers them. Finally, let them express all feelings—even the most negative ones. If they feel frustrated because they accidentally broke a toy and start crying, let them vent. Avoid constantly intervening and solving problems for your child, but teach them how all emotions count and help them grow.

Techniques to Foster a Deep Connection From Birth

Boosting your child's emotional development also involves fostering a deep connection from birth. The most effective technique to build a long-lasting bond with your child is to be physically close and talk to them. We'll look at both of them in the following sections.

Kangaroo Care: The Power of Skin-To-Skin Contact

Have you ever heard about kangaroo care or skin-to-skin contact? They're used to identify the act of holding your baby to your chest. To properly practice kangaroo care, your baby must only wear their diaper and socks to stay warm, and you must hold them close to your bare chest. Therefore, your skins touch each other. You can practice kangaroo care in a hospital or at home and do it as often as you want. Except for the fact that your skin must touch your child's, there's no particular rule. However, you can follow some easy tips to make sure you properly practice skin-to-skin contact. You must dress comfortably to feel more relaxed and place your baby's head on one side against your chest. When you've found the perfect position for you and your child, you must keep them warm by covering them with a blanket. To practice kangaroo care effectively, you must relax as much as possible. Take deep breaths, let your baby sleep, and don't play with them. Whenever you practice skin-to-skin contact, you must have enough time to dedicate to your child and regularly repeat it to ensure you create a deep emotional bond with them. Conversely, you must avoid some unhealthy behaviors during kangaroo care. For example, you shouldn't do it when you're sick or if your skin isn't clean and healthy. You mustn't smoke, and you must put all the distractions away, such as electronic devices (*Kangaroo Care*, 2020).

The benefits of kangaroo care don't only include fostering a deep connection with your baby but also improving their physical health. In fact, practicing skin-to-skin contact can encourage healthy sleep and your baby's growth. Moreover, it can regularize their breathing, as they learn to keep your pace and breathe regularly, and stabilize their heart rate. Keeping your baby close to you during some medical procedures can also alleviate their pain. If you're skeptical about kangaroo care, keep in mind research has often proved all its positive effects on babies' physical health and parents' relationship with them (*Kangaroo Care*, 2020). To witness all the benefits skin-to-skin contact has, you must begin practicing it as soon as possible. Research has found that there's the so-called "golden hour," which is the perfect time to maximize your bond with your baby through kangaroo care (*All About Skin-To-Skin Contact*, 2017). The golden hour corresponds with the first hour of your child's life. If you can, you should try skin-to-skin contact with your baby as soon as they're born. This way, you'll be more likely to create a deep connection with them.

The Art of Talking: Even if They Can't Talk Back, Babies Are Listening

You might favor touch over other forms of communication with your baby because you know they can't talk. You might believe speaking to your child when they are just born or only a few months old is too soon because they can't understand your words. Obviously, toddlers can't grasp the meaning of every word you say, but they surely appreciate your voice. Your baby will pay attention to your language and how you talk to them. For example, they'll be particularly attracted by the typical baby talk, which includes speaking slowly and using simple phrases with an exaggerated tone. Research has shown that toddlers are fast learners and can learn 10 or even more words every day (Singh et al., 2018). Therefore, you must try to speak to them as much as possible.

Talking to your baby has many long-term benefits. For instance, it can increase their vocabulary. Your baby will look at your face while you speak and try to imitate your mouth's movement. This way, they'll quickly learn to repeat your words. The more words you talk to them, the more they'll understand. Moreover, your baby will calm down when hearing your voice, especially if you sing to them. They'll also improve other skills that will be essential for the rest of their life, such as language, thinking, math, social, and reading skills (Singh et al., 2018). As you can see, using your voice to interact with your child can have a life-long impact on their development.

How can you talk to your baby? You must take advantage of every moment to communicate your feelings, thoughts, and emotions with them and describe your baby's environment. Whenever you're about to do something with them, you can clearly communicate it. For example, you can tell your baby something like, "Let's go take a bath!" Remember to always maintain eye contact with them, gently talk to them, and respond to reactions such as cooing or babbling. It's important to give feedback to your baby to let them understand you appreciate their effort to communicate with you. You must also smile at them to make them feel secure and loved and play games, like peek-a-boo. You must also try to sing instead of just talking to them, as babies naturally grasp rhythm and can learn more rapidly. You might feel uncomfortable and awkward when you start singing to your baby, but you must keep practicing until you feel at ease. To foster a deep connection with your baby and positive development, you must also take time to read to them every day. Until recently, reading stories to children was considered a purely maternal activity. However, fathers can read stories, too. Don't be afraid to accompany your baby to bed and read something to them.

The Importance of Touch, Talk, and Play

Touch: The Primal Power of Hugging, Cuddling, or Even a Simple Pat

As you already learned in the section about kangaroo care, touch is essential to foster positive development in your child. That's why you mustn't only practice skin-to-skin care but encourage all forms of physical contact with your baby. Keep in mind you can promote physical contact in various ways; the most important thing is that you touch them with care, patience, and love. You must transmit the message that you love them unconditionally and accept them as they are. You can hug or cuddle them or even give them a simple pat on the shoulder. It doesn't matter how you create physical contact—you must always show love.

Thanks to your touch, your baby learns to regulate their emotions and properly handle stress (*Hold Me Close*, 2021). For example, you can hold them in your arms or rock them when you notice they feel stressed or anxious. This way, you'll help them soothe and calm down. As you repeat the same behavior to make them feel relaxed, they learn what they can do to calm down in stressful situations. In other words, they learn to self-regulate thanks to your touch. If you teach your child to regulate their emotions, they're also more likely to understand other people's emotions, too. Therefore, they can build strong and close relationships with the people they'll meet during their lives. Studies have also shown that both mothers' and fathers' touch can wire their child's brain to success in social situations. Results have confirmed that nurturing and gentle touch stimulates areas of the brain connected with emotional and social development. This means that physical contact with your baby at an early stage promotes effective interactions with other people when they grow up (*Hold Me Close*, 2021).

The above studies suggest you must promote physical contact with your child as soon as they're born. Whenever you have time, hold your baby, hug them, or cuddle them. Show them you take care of them with a gentle touch.

Talk: Building Their Vocabulary and Understanding of the World

Previously, we briefly introduced all the advantages and ways in which you can talk to your baby. Now, let's look at them in depth. Many studies have found that talking to and reading to your child has an incredibly positive effect on their language and vocabulary (Sample, 2014). Even when babies are just 18 months old, you can easily see the difference between a baby whose parents speak to them frequently and one whose parents don't. When they're 24 months old, children with a poorer vocabulary start lagging behind their peers. Chatting with your baby helps them understand the rules and rhythms of language, thus making it easier for them to recognize and learn new words. The more you talk to them, the more they properly process language and learn words. Some studies have found that not talking to your baby might hinder their success at school. In fact, they might possess a less developed vocabulary and lag in memory and verbal skills. Researchers have also discovered that babies develop language more quickly when their parents discuss topics that interest them. Therefore, make sure to have long and deep conversations about which toy to buy next or what to eat for dinner. Researchers have also found that replacing a conversation with a TV or iPad doesn't produce the same results (Sample, 2014).

However, you might still wonder what you should focus on: Quality or quantity? In other words, is it better to teach as many words as possible to your child every day or to focus on the quality of your conversation with them? Studies have found that quality is much more important (Canzater, 2019). The main difference between quantity and quality consists of your baby's involvement. When you favor quantity, you teach them a lot of words without engaging them in a real conversation. When you favor quality, you actively involve your baby and let them participate in the discussion, even if they can't say much. Moreover, quality also includes using more encouraging than discouraging words. If you aim at teaching many words, you might often repeat something like, "No, this is not how you pronounce it," which only makes your child feel bad and doesn't encourage them to try harder. Conversely, appreciating their effort before explaining their mistake makes them feel better. To help your child quickly and effectively develop their language, you must focus on the quality of your conversations with them.

Play: The Joy and Developmental Benefits of Engaging in Simple Games

To promote your child's development, you mustn't only focus on touching and talking to them but also on playing. Babies love playing, and you can take advantage of it to show them how the world works and teach them new things in a funny way. When your baby is just born, they won't be able to play many games. However, you can always try peek-a-boo with them. Peek-a-boo is an incredibly simple game that helps your child develop object permanence, approach learning positively, and boost social skills (*Peek A Boo*, 2017). Object permanence is the ability to understand that an object still exists even if you can't see it. This is a fundamental concept your baby will need to develop properly. Thanks to peek-a-boo, your child can also appreciate learning by being actively engaged and involved in a game. Finally, playing peek-a-boo allows your child to understand how to take turns and respect others during playtime. This last benefit will be particularly important when they start going to school and sharing with other children.

The most classical way of playing peek-a-boo is by asking your baby, "Where am I?" while you cover your face with your hands. Wait for a few seconds, then take your hands off your face and say, "Peek-a-boo! Here I am!" Alternatively, you can play peek-a-boo with an object. Choose an item that is small and easy to hide under a cloth. Show the object to your baby and let them explore it for a few seconds or minutes. Then, hide it under a cloth and ask your baby, "Where is the object?" Wait for some time and pull the cloth off to show them the item was always there. When you first try peek-a-boo, your baby will be surprised and fascinated by the game. They look at you in surprise, wondering how the object could disappear and magically reappear. When they start developing object permanence, they understand you're hiding your face under your hands and the object under the cloth.

Playing is an essential part of raising your child. Make sure to always save some time to play with your child to promote their emotional and physical development. Just a few minutes every day after coming back from work will be enough to show your baby you care about them and feel like interacting with them.

Interactive Element

When your baby starts talking, you'll feel excited and proud of them. You'll feel a joy you've probably never felt before and will want to keep track of their progress. As you learned, fostering language development by talking to your child is essential for their development. Therefore, make sure to dedicate a few minutes every day to teach them a few words (one new word can be enough) and remember that quality is more important than quantity. You can keep track of your baby's progress in various ways. You will find an example of a sheet you can use daily below and how to fill it in. As you can see, you just have to insert the date your baby spoke, the words they said, and where they said it. Then, explain why they felt the need to say that word. For example, you can write down what questions you asked them. Finally, you can also insert notes, if your baby did something remarkable.

Date	Word/word approximation	Where was it spoken?	Strategy used	Notes
04/10	"wawa" (water)	During lunch	I asked my baby if they wanted water or milk.	Responded quickly

In this chapter, we learned the importance of a deep emotional bond with our children and how to foster it from the day they're born. We discovered our children's main needs and how being a good example can make them learn appropriate behaviors more quickly. Then, we learned about the importance of touch, talk, and play. Practicing kangaroo care and talking to our children helps us create a deep connection with them. We can also try to sing to them, read books, and play peek-a-boo, which helps them understand essential concepts and properly develop. Finally, we looked at a sheet we can use to track down the words our babies say. Now that we've dived deep into the heart of emotional bonding let's step back and look at the broader picture. The art of juggling: How does one balance the demands of work with the joys and responsibilities of family? Let's navigate this balancing act in the next chapter.

4

Balancing Act—Work and Family

Imagine life as a game in which you are juggling some five balls in the air. You name them: work, family, health, friends, and spirit—and you're keeping all of these in the air. You will soon understand that work is a rubber ball. If you drop it, it will bounce back. But the other four balls—family, health, friends, and spirit—are made of glass. If you drop one of these, they will be irrevocably scuffed, marked, nicked, damaged, or even shattered. They will never be the same. You must understand that and strive for balance in your life.

Brian Dyson

As Brian Dyson, the former President and CEO of Coca-Cola Enterprises, teaches us, balancing work and family might be challenging. However, we must always choose family over work because we can always find a new job, but we can't always repair broken relationships. However, this doesn't mean we should abandon our jobs or not consider them an important part of our lives. In fact, we must find the perfect work-life balance to feel satisfied both at work and at home. In this chapter, we'll learn how to prioritize family without forgetting work responsibilities and discover some valuable tips to manage time properly. Next, we'll learn how to set boundaries at work and properly communicate them to our bosses and coworkers. Finally, we'll look at a time management sheet we can use to check the time we allocate to work and family.

Prioritizing Family While Fulfilling Work Responsibilities

Work-life balance is the relationship between your job and all other aspects of your life, such as your family, spouse, friends, relatives, and activities you enjoy doing in your free time. If you have a good work-life balance, it means you manage to allocate enough time to all essential areas of your life. A well-balanced life improves your mental, physical, and emotional energy, boosts your happiness, and reduces the probability of suffering from burnout and stress (*Work-Life Balance*, 2021). If you dedicate too much time to work, you might feel like you're neglecting your family. Therefore, you might feel unsatisfied. At the same time, you might want more with your significant other because you're always too busy to have time for them and your children. Consequently, you feel stressed—the more stressed you feel, the less energy you have to care for your children. As you can see, poor work-life balance might hinder your relationship with your partner and baby.

If you're afraid you might develop a poor work-life balance once your baby is born, you can already do something to avoid future problems. Even if you already have a child and need some help adjusting your work-life balance, you can follow some practical tips. First of all, you must always remember quality is more important than quantity. Even if you're busy and can't spend a lot of hours every day taking care of your partner and baby, you can still spend some quality time together. If you come home late, you can still ask how their day was and take a few seconds to say hi to your baby and hold or hug them. Smile at them and tell them something nice with a high-pitched voice so they understand you want to communicate your happiness to them. You can always take a few minutes every day to focus on your family. It might sound hard in the beginning, but you'll easily get used to it. If you think about it, our significant others and children already get our leftover energy, as we tend to focus more on work and duties. Therefore, try not to use up all your batteries and leave a bit of emotional and mental energy for your family.

In addition to focusing on quality instead of quantity, you can also integrate healthy habits into your life. If you're not used to planning and scheduling, I suggest you start right now, especially if you run your own business and don't consistently finish work at the same time. Start by choosing the right moment of the day to sit down and plan what you will do next. You can dedicate a few minutes every morning to writing down what you want to do during the day and check if you completed all the tasks of the previous days. Alternatively, you can set aside a few minutes after your baby has fallen asleep or before you go to bed to plan the activities you need to do the next day. Remember to include not only your duties but also your hobbies and the activities you practice in your free time. This way, you'll be able to schedule some time to focus on your family, too. It's also important to understand the difference between negotiable and nonnegotiable things. If you want to find the perfect balance between family and work, prepare to sacrifice something. At some point, you'll have to choose among all the tasks and activities you must accomplish. Let's say you're used to receiving many calls from work, even after you've left your office and arrived home. To find the perfect balance, you might decide not to answer calls after 7 p.m. so that you can completely dedicate yourself to your family. If you're used to traveling often and attending in-person meetings, you might decide to work from home or attend fewer meetings when possible.

The fundamental tip you must always follow is to take some time for yourself to focus on your mental health. Stop believing you'll never have time for yourself because you can do it if you properly schedule it and feel motivated. Remember, your mental health has a huge impact on your baby's overall well-being. If you neglect yourself, you might feel stressed and overwhelmed by your duties. Your baby might feel your distress and be negatively influenced by it. To avoid such situations, take a few minutes every day to do something you enjoy—even just singing or listening to your favorite songs while going to work.

Time Management Tips for the Busy Dad

Learning to manage your time properly is the most effective way of balancing work and life. It doesn't matter if you're already a father or waiting for your baby's arrival—the following time management techniques can help you keep track of the time you allocate to your work and family. In fact, such techniques can save your life on many occasions. Just give them a try and choose the one that better suits your needs.

Time blocking is a time management technique that helps you divide your day into blocks. Most people don't properly divide all the tasks they have to complete. For example, you might have to regularly check your emails to answer customers or coworkers. If you don't use time blocking, you might keep checking your email whenever you have time, like after a few minutes, an hour, after lunch, and then again after a few minutes, and so on. You might also decide to spread out all your meetings throughout the day. Therefore, you might meet early in the morning, one before lunch, and another in the afternoon. If you practice time blocking, you learn to dedicate an established amount of time to all similar tasks. For example, you can check your emails just twice a day, before having lunch and before the end of your working day. You can also try to schedule all your meetings in the same block, like in the afternoon from 2 p.m. to 5 p.m. As already mentioned, you must also dedicate a few minutes every day to plan your upcoming activities so that you know how you'll divide your time into blocks.

Another useful time management technique is called the Pomodoro technique. The term "Pomodoro" is the Italian word for "tomato." In fact, the Pomodoro technique was invented by the Italian entrepreneur Francesco Cirillo in the late 1980s (Sheldon, 2022). At that time, he was studying at the university and needed to find a technique to maximize his time. Therefore, he used a tomato-shaped kitchen timer to organize his time. After some trial and error, he finally realized that the perfect time to focus on a task was 25 minutes (or 25 pomodori). He thought that less than 25 minutes wasn't enough to complete a task, while more than 25 was too much to keep the focus. If you want to try the Pomodoro technique, you must plan your tasks so that you can dedicate just 25 minutes at a time to them. After 25 minutes, stop for 2 to 5 minutes and then start again. Repeat this cycle 4 times, then, take a longer break of 15 to 30 minutes. The result will be that you will spend about 2 hours focused on your tasks with a total break of 20 minutes. Then, you rest a bit longer and start again. I would suggest you use the Pomodoro technique to manage your work time and not the other aspects of your life, as it is specifically created to tackle demanding tasks. If you want, you can try using the time-blocking technique discussed above to organize your time with your family and other activities not related to your work.

Finally, the Eisenhower matrix is another popular and effective time management technique. The Eisenhower matrix comprises of four quadrants where you divide the tasks you want to accomplish daily. Urgent and vital tasks usually have deadlines and are of high significance for you. Urgent and not essential duties concern organizing and planning your time, such as reflecting on long-term projects. Not urgent, but important assignments can be emails or calls, which you must answer as soon as you can but aren't essential in your life. Finally, not urgent and not important tasks include the activities you do in your free time that don't improve your life, such as hanging out with your coworkers.

To properly manage your time, you must always organize in a way that you can take a break every now and then. In fact, nobody manages to maintain focus on the same task for a long time. Then, make sure to stop focusing when the timer goes off, even if you've not completed the task or accomplished what you expected.

Setting Boundaries at Work for Family Time

Previously, we mentioned we need to sacrifice something if we want to find the perfect balance between work and family. For example, you might need to stop answering calls once you arrive home after work. On one hand, it might be easy, as you just need to turn your phone off or leave it somewhere it won't disturb you. On the other hand, it means you must set boundaries with your colleagues, customers, and superiors to make them understand you allocate a limited time to work and you're not always available. Boundaries are limits we must establish in all sorts of relationships—even with our partners—and define the behaviors we accept and don't accept. Telling your colleagues you don't answer calls after 7 p.m. is setting a boundary with them. Setting boundaries not only helps you balance life and work but also reduces conflicts, builds healthy relationships, and enhances communication. If your colleagues know what you want from them, they'll be more likely to accept it and engage in the appropriate behaviors. They'll also feel more comfortable with you, and you'll be able to communicate your needs properly. As setting boundaries is essential for your overall well-being, learning how to do it can also encourage your child to do the same. If they see you setting your boundaries and respecting others, they'll be likelier to do the same as adults.

How can you set boundaries at work? First, you must reflect on your values, beliefs, and goals, and you must figure out what your boundaries are. You can't communicate your limits to others if you don't know what they are. If you want, you can discuss your values with your loved one and think about a way to handle work that can benefit both of you. You can ask for their advice or feedback on your behavior to know if they have already identified some unhealthy habits you can eliminate. After understanding your boundaries, you must communicate them to your coworkers and superiors. Let's take the previous examples of the calls after 7 p.m. You can gather your colleagues and tell them from that moment onward you won't accept calls after 7 p.m. Alternatively, you can explain your behavior the day after to each colleague who tries to call you. You can tell them something like, "I want to dedicate more time to my family, so I prefer not answering calls after 7 p.m. Would it be possible for you to wait until the next day to tell me what you need to, or maybe send me a message instead of calling?"

You mustn't be afraid of telling your coworkers how much you care about your family and want to be present with them.

After communicating your boundaries, prepare to wait in order to let your coworkers and superiors adjust to the change. They might keep calling you after 7 p.m. for a while, and then, finally, they will understand you won't answer them. In case a colleague or superior insists on calling you, you must re-assert your boundaries and repeat to them that you need some time for your family. Learn to defend yourself and your values, and protect your boundaries. Therefore, you must learn to say "No." If you struggle to decline offers, you might practice saying "No" by rejecting insignificant requests. Make sure to always be polite and express appreciation for the offer. Then, gently reject it. If you want, you can add a reason to make others understand why you behave like that, but it's not necessary. You can just say something like, "I'd be happy to handle this project, but I'm already busy and can't work more hours because I have to take care of my child." To make sure you maintain a healthy relationship with your colleagues and superiors, take some time off. Take advantage of all the available days off, or take a break from time to time if you run your own business. Make sure to schedule days off and use them to relax.

Interactive Element

If you need help managing your time, you can start using the sheets below. In the first one, you'll find an activity log where you can record each activity you must accomplish, its duration, and the total hours you want to dedicate to it each week and month. This way, you'll be able to keep track of your progress on each task and adjust the time you allocate to it in case you don't manage to follow your initial plans. In the second sheet, you'll look at a daily checklist that helps you prioritize tasks. You can divide assignments based on their priority. If you want, you can use the Eisenhower matrix we discussed in this chapter to distinguish between important and not important tasks. You can use both sheets to keep track of all the activities you want to do: Work, family, friends, hobbies, and so on. If you wish, you can also create different activity logs and daily checklists depending on the aspect of your life they refer to.

Activity Log

Activity description	Duration	Weekly totals	Monthly totals
Playing with my child	10 minutes per day	70 minutes	Between 4 and 5 hours
Completing a project	1 week	32 hours	1 week

Daily Checklist

High Priority

- Going grocery shopping
-
-
-

Medium Priority

- Calling a customer for a future project
-
-
-

Low Priority

- Having a drink with my coworkers
-
-
-

In this chapter, we learned everything we need to balance work and life properly. We must find ways to prioritize family over work, as neglecting the former might have negative long-term effects. To find the perfect work-life balance, we must prioritize quality over quantity time with our families and integrate healthy habits into our daily lives. We must also practice useful time management techniques, like time blocking, the Pomodoro technique, and the Eisenhower matrix. Finally, we must set healthy boundaries at work to make our colleagues and superiors understand how important our families are. In this chapter, we learned to balance work and life. But what about your relationship? In the next chapter, we'll delve into how to be a supportive partner while navigating the ups and downs of fatherhood.

5

Keeping Love Strong Amidst Baby Bliss

The strength of a family, like the strength of an army, lies in its loyalty to each other.

Mario Puzo

Once your baby is born, you might have mixed feelings. On one hand, you might feel excited and ready to start a new chapter in your life together with your partner. On the other hand, you might feel excluded and left out. You might notice your relationship with your partner is entirely different now that you have a baby, and you might feel jealous or neglected. Consequently, you might feel guilty for not loving your child as much as you thought and having negative feelings. However, you might not know most fathers feel the same way. Being a father changes everything, so we all need some time to adjust. We might all feel a bit jealous of our children who take up all of the attention and care. That's why you must learn to accept those negative feelings and move on with your life to ensure a strong and deep connection with your significant other. In this chapter, you'll learn how your relationship might change when the baby's born and how to maintain an open channel of communication after pregnancy. You'll also learn everything you need to know about the main physical and emotional changes your partner will undergo after the baby's arrival. This way, you'll know how to handle the situation and avoid feeling left out. Finally, you'll find a practical activity to check in with your loved one and the state of your relationship.

The Changing Dynamics of a Relationship Post-Baby

As a first-time dad, you might not feel an emotional bond with your baby during the early stages of their life. Some time ago, I read a story of a father who was 26 years old and had a wonderful, healthy relationship with their partner. They extensively discussed having a baby, and after careful reflection, they decided it was the right time, and they were both ready. The father was a bit more reticent, but he was still excited to become a dad and start his own family. After his baby was born, he didn't feel love but hatred. He considered himself a loving and kind person and couldn't explain why he couldn't love his own child.

The father didn't know mixed feelings are quite common among first-time dads, so he felt insecure, worried, and inadequate. He felt something was wrong with him because he believed all fathers immediately love their children. However, that's not always the case. Jealousy and other negative feelings are quite common among both parents. It means even your mother-to-be might feel envious or bad. But why does it happen? Research shows that having fears of rejection or abandonment or relationship anxiety might trigger negative feelings in the soon-to-be parent (Olsson, 2022). That's because they might already struggle with doubts, fears, and uncertainties inside the relationship, and having a baby who takes all the attention might be extremely stressful and challenging. In fact, it might bring up repressed emotions or thoughts that strain the relationship. If you both experience negative emotions, like jealousy, you might end up fighting all the time and yelling at each other. Consequently, your tense relationship might affect your child's health and well-being. Studies suggest that after having a baby, almost 70% of couples experience a decline in relationship satisfaction (Olsson, 2022). Therefore, childbirth might have long-term and negative effects on your relationship.

A few years ago, an interesting study was conducted to test the effects of childbirth on relationship satisfaction (Grabmeier, 2020). Mothers and fathers answered some questions during the third trimester of pregnancy to understand their levels of relationship anxiety. They were asked if they feared losing their other's love or feeling abandoned. Three months after childbirth, parents had to answer questions about their relationship with their partner and baby. For example, they had to say if they felt resentful toward their other parent when they dedicated more time and attention to their child. Those who had higher levels of relationship anxiety before the baby's arrival were also more likely to feel negative emotions, like jealousy and resentment, after childbirth. Surprisingly, spouses with an anxious partner also felt high levels of jealousy. How's that possible? Researchers think that those who were anxious were used to receiving a lot of attention before the child's arrival. After the birth, they not only received less attention but all their devotion was completely focused on their baby (Grabmeier, 2020).

Now, you might believe fathers experience more relationship anxiety before childbirth and are more likely to feel jealous after the baby's arrival. That's not what researchers found (Grabmeier, 2020). In fact, both mothers and fathers who felt anxious before having a child were more likely to feel jealous after their baby was born. Mothers can also be envious of the time fathers spend with their babies, especially if they're really involved (Grabmeier, 2020). You might also believe you're doomed to strain your relationship and might regret the idea of having a baby. However, you can start working on your relationship now and prepare yourself to face challenging times once your baby arrives. To ensure your relationship remains healthy and positive, you must effectively communicate with them and understand the emotional and physical changes they will undergo after childbirth.

Strategies for Effective Communication

Let's start with effective communication. Effective communication is an essential skill we should all have to strive for in life. Therefore, you might need it in different aspects of your life, and you might want to develop it in any case. What do you think effective communication entails? You might believe it means properly expressing your thoughts and feelings, not attacking the other person, using kind words, and so on. Obviously, you must learn to communicate what's happening inside of you to effectively communicate, but you must also do something more important: listen. Do you always carefully listen to what they tell you? If not, why? When others talk to us, we generally don't listen to every word they say because we easily lose concentration. We might prepare what will say next, think about a different topic, get distracted by other people and things around us, or mind our own business. Carefully listening is much harder than you might think.

You must understand the difference between passive listening or hearing and active listening. When you passively listen to your partner, you just hear their words but don't elaborate on them or retain the message they want to send you. For example, your partner might tell you to put your dishes in the dishwasher, and you might even reply, "Yes," but you forget what they said the minute after. Therefore, you don't do what they have asked you, and they might get upset. When you actively listen, you show your partner you understood their message. For instance, you might ask them something like, "Do you prefer I put my dishes in the dishwasher right now, or can I first finish this task?" As you can see, this sentence shows you have clearly understood what your partner has told you and have reacted to their message by asking a question to clarify how you should put their request into practice. Active listening can truly improve your relationship by reducing conflicts. If you listen to your partner, you understand what they want from you, and can satisfy their needs. They can do the same with you. Consequently, you can also identify and solve problems more easily, thus creating a strong and deep connection with each other.

How can you become better at actively listening? First, you mustn't talk at the same time. Especially when emotions are running high, you might talk over them. When this happens, you can't understand what they are saying and can't collaborate to solve the problem. If you see they need to talk and express their opinion, let them. Listen to their words and take a few seconds to reflect on what they said. In fact, you shouldn't let your emotions run wild and say things you might immediately regret. Think about what they have told you and how you would like to reply. Take their feelings into consideration and try not to hurt them. To properly answer, you must also try to put yourself in their shoes. Even if you've been together and known each other for years, you might still struggle to grasp their point of view. Take a few seconds to think about how they might feel and what they might think.

To avoid conflicts and effectively communicate your thoughts and feelings, you must also stick to the facts and leave the past in the past. If you think they are lying to you but lack evidence to confirm this, just consider what truly matters and forget about your doubts. If you're 100% sure they are lying, when they're actually not, you might create more conflict and misunderstanding. Moreover, you must leave the past behind during conversations and not bring up things that happened weeks, months, or years before. Especially when you have a baby, you might keep track of all the things you do for them, like waking up in the middle of the night. At some point, you might decide to rub your effort in their face when they don't do something for you. As you might guess, this is not an effective way of communicating what you want and need from them. They might feel attacked, get upset, and start an unnecessary argument. Remember, being a part of a couple doesn't mean equally dividing tasks and duties because it's impossible. For some time, you might put more effort and energy into the relationship while they don't. Then, you exchange roles, and they put in more effort. Never forget about the times they were there for you.

Understanding the Emotional and Physical Changes in Your Partner

To maintain a good relationship, you must become aware of the main changes they might undergo after giving birth to your child. In Chapter 1, we quickly looked at some of the most common physical and emotional changes, but now we'll delve into them.

As for physical changes, you might already know about common ones, like loose skin and stretch marks, which usually go away after some time and don't have too much influence on their body image. However, other changes are permanent and can provoke negative feelings. If they choose to breastfeed, their breasts might undergo significant changes: They might increase in size during the breastfeeding phase and then decrease afterward (Migala, 2023). That's because the alveoli in their breasts that produce milk shrink after the breastfeeding period ends. Another permanent change concerns shoe size. As they gain weight during pregnancy, their feet might increase in length, thus provoking a gain of about half a shoe size. That happens because they carry your baby for about nine months, which means they carry more weight than their feet are used to. During pregnancy, they might have the impression they have more hair than usual. Well, that's not false. In fact, increased levels of hormones might reduce hair loss during pregnancy. After childbirth, they might complain they're losing a lot of hair, but they're just losing what they didn't lose during pregnancy. Moreover, a woman's hips enlarge when they give birth to a child, and they might never return to their previous shape. Finally, their menstrual periods might be different. If they don't breastfeed, their periods will reappear six to eight months after childbirth and might be heavier. They might feel much more fatigued, tired, and weak; they might need to change pads every hour or so, and they might have large blood clots (Migala, 2023).

As you might guess, all these physical changes might provoke negative emotions in your partner. They might feel anxious and frustrated by all the daily changes they must undergo. They might also feel stressed because of the new responsibilities they have as a parent. They might even develop postpartum depression, which affects about 8 to 17% of all mothers (Pedersen et al., 2021). The name of the mental health disorder derives from the fact that most mothers develop it after giving birth to their child, although it might also appear during pregnancy (Horsager-Boehrer, 2015). Postpartum depression includes feeling sad most of the time, having difficulties sleeping and concentrating, having suicidal thoughts, and losing interest in all the hobbies and activities mothers enjoyed before. However, mothers can also suffer from simple "baby blues," which are short periods when they feel a bit sadder than usual. You can easily distinguish baby blues from postpartum depression, as the former are less severe and don't influence their feelings and thoughts as much as the latter (Horsager-Boehrer, 2015).

At the beginning of this chapter, you learned that you could feel negative emotions toward your child, just like your partner can. You probably didn't know it, but you might also suffer from postpartum depression. Research has found that 1 in 10 dads might struggle with such a mental health disorder (Horsager-Boehrer, 2021). Moreover, fathers' postpartum depression might negatively affect their relationship with others and the baby's health. In fact, the child might be more likely to develop mental and physical health problems, might be neglected, and might engage in risky and unhealthy behaviors as an adult (Horsager-Boehrer, 2021). As you can see, fathers' mental health is as important as mothers'. Therefore, you must take care of yourself. Just like mothers, fathers can develop postpartum depression even before the child is born, and various reasons might cause it. A father is more likely to suffer from postpartum depression if their partner also suffers from it, if they have a family history of depression, if they don't sleep enough, and if they struggle to adjust to parenthood. However, other issues like relationship or financial problems can also provoke the onset of postpartum depression. Pay attention to some common symptoms you might notice, like irritability or even bursts of anger, loss of motivation, increase in impulsive behavior, poor concentration, and frequent headaches or stomach aches (Horsager-Boehrer, 2021).

Interactive Element

In Chapter 2, we looked at some prompts you can use to cultivate a positive and growth mindset before your baby's arrival. Now, we'll look at more prompts to check in on your relationship and make sure you maintain a strong and positive connection with them. Remember to dedicate just a few minutes every day to ask how they feel and note down if you notice some changes. Then, think about ways you can improve the situation. For the moment, you can start by answering the following questions and reflecting on your relationship in general.

- Write down how you would define a healthy and an unhealthy relationship and how you would distinguish them.
- Do you think your relationship is currently working?
- Think about the pros and cons of being in love: What do you find challenging and rewarding?
- What can you do every day to make your partner feel better?

- How can you be more grateful for your significant other?
- How can you show more love?
- Write down 10 special things about your partner.
- Write down 10 special things about your relationship.
- What values do you want to communicate in your relationship, and how do you express them? For example, how do you communicate honesty or respect?
- What does "family" mean to you?
- Is there something you would like to improve in your relationship? If so, what and how would you improve it?
- What do you expect from your relationship?
- Do you accept your partner for who they are?

As you can read, the above questions are just about you and your significant other. In fact, you must always remember to dedicate a few minutes every day just to them and your relationship. It doesn't mean you're being selfish, but you're taking care of them and your mental health.

In this chapter, we focused on the relationship with our significant other. We discovered we must prepare ourselves for changes that might occur and affect our relationships. When our babies arrive, we might feel jealous or resentful because our partners are completely devoted to them and leave us behind. We mustn't feel guilty because those feelings are common, and we must put effort into maintaining a healthy relationship. To do so, we must learn to communicate effectively by actively listening to them and understand and accept their physical and emotional changes. We must also pay attention to postpartum depression. Finally, we looked at some useful prompts to help us work on our relationship. We can use them as a starting point to dedicate some time to the relationship with our spouses. Now that we've tackled the art of being supportive, let's delve into the myriad of challenges that come with the title of 'Dad.' From sleepless nights to deciphering baby cries, the next chapter will arm us with tools to overcome the common hurdles of new fatherhood.

Make a Difference with Your Dad Review

Unlock the Power of Fatherhood

"The heart of a father is the masterpiece of nature."

Antoine François Prévost d'Exiles

Remember that time when she said, "I'm pregnant..." and your world shifted? The rollercoaster of emotions, from excitement to nervousness. It was a new journey, and just like you sought guidance, many others will too. They'll need a road map, some reassurance, and maybe a dash of humor.

Do you recall that feeling of wishing you had a guidebook, tailored just for dads? A blueprint that said it's okay to be clueless at first, but also shared the nitty-gritty on dirty diapers, late nights, and those precious baby giggles?

The magic is in shared experiences. Knowing that someone has walked the path before and survived (with a few stains and lots of laughs).

Would you be willing to shine a light for a soon-to-be dad, wandering, just like you once were?

Becoming a father is a gift, an adventure, a challenge, and a joy. Our goal is to make this journey into fatherhood accessible to everyone. Your experiences, combined with the wisdom in this book, can become a beacon.

I humbly request your help. Be the guiding star for another dad out there. Most people do, in fact, judge a book by its cover (and its reviews). So, leave a review, share your story, and let's help another first-time dad out there.

Your review might just be...

...a beacon during a sleepless night.
...a laugh during a stressful day.
...an answer to an unsaid prayer.
...a guide during a confusing phase.
...and most importantly, a hand to say, "You got this, Dad!"

To share the love, the laughs, and the lessons, all you need to do is...

★ ★ ★ ★ ★

If you are on audible - hit the three dots in the top right of your device, click rate & review, then leave a few sentences about the book with a star rating.

If you are reading on kindle or an e-reader - scroll to the bottom of the book, then swipe up and it will prompt a review for you.

If for some reason these changed - you can go to Amazon (or wherever you purchased this) and leave a review right on the book's page.

If all fails, scan this QR code or visit this link - https://www.a-mazon.com/review/create-review/?asin=B0CXGFF4JR

You are an awesome dad! Keep being the best dad you can be!

Thank you from the bottom of my heart.

~ Your biggest fan, Dante

PS: If you provide something of value to another person, it makes you more valuable to them. If you'd like goodwill straight from another dad – and you believe this book will help them – send this book their way.

6

Overcoming Common Challenges of New Fatherhood

D id you know that fathers lose about 44 days of sleep during the first year of their baby's life (Marcoux, 2017)? At least, that's what research in the UK has found out. You might have heard other fathers complain about being tired and overly fatigued. You might have heard dreadful stories about fathers who put their car keys in the fridge or often forget what they must do. Well, those are the effects of sleep deprivation, which is almost inevitable, especially during your child's first year of life. A study has found that parents lose about two hours of sleep every night during the first five months of their baby and one hour per night until they turn 2 (Marcoux, 2017). As you might guess, sleep deprivation can have a negative impact on your overall well-being. If you don't get enough sleep for a prolonged period, you might struggle to concentrate, gain weight, have accidents, perform poorly at work, and get sick more often. For all these reasons, you must learn to take care of yourself and address the most common problems all fathers share. In this chapter, you'll learn some practical and valuable tips to rest better, how to face typical fears and anxieties of being a parent, and how to ask for help from other fathers. Finally, a workable activity at the end of this chapter will help you become aware of and analyze your feelings.

Sleep Deprivation: Tips for Better Rest

Although sleep deprivation concerns both parents, a study has found that fathers might get less sleep than mothers (Haelle & Willingham, 2019). Why? Fathers usually manage to sleep a bit more during the night because they don't have to wake up to feed the baby, as mothers have to. However, mothers have the opportunity to catch up during the daytime, while fathers can't. This means that fathers don't have as much of an opportunity to recover the lost hours of sleep. In addition to clear impacts on mental and physical health, sleep deprivation might also have negative consequences for the relationship with your partner. Research has discovered that men tend to overestimate their partners' moodiness, while women believe fathers sleep much more than they actually do (Haelle & Willingham, 2019). Such prejudices and misconceptions might lead to useless arguments where mothers accuse fathers of sleeping too much, and fathers blame the mother for feeling too moody.

As hard as it might be in the first few months of your baby's life, you must always remember things will get better. As your child keeps growing, you'll gradually be able to sleep more and more. However, you mustn't undervalue the negative effects sleep deprivation can have in those first few months. That's why you must find ways to get some sleep in one way or another. One tip you can follow is to use power naps and take advantage of them when your baby falls asleep. In general, a newborn baby needs about 16 to 18 hours of sleep during the day, which is when you should take advantage of resting (Majendie, n.d.). However, their sleep pattern is not as exact as yours, so they randomly fall asleep during the day. Take advantage of those moments and rest for a while. Go to bed to get some rest or use a comfortable sofa. You can also create a good sleep environment by buying an eye mask to use during the day, using earplugs, or keeping comfortable pillows and blankets handy. This way, you'll always have what you need near you to get some proper sleep.

Do you remember in Chapter 4 how you learned how to set boundaries at work? You can do the same to get some rest. In the first few months, all your friends and relatives might be excited and curious to finally meet the baby. You must learn to kindly say "No" and assure them that they'll be able to see your child later on. If you set healthy boundaries with your loved ones, you can take advantage of all the available moments you have to rest and relax instead of chatting with friends and relatives. Even if you love them, you might feel exhausted and overwhelmed by talking to them, especially if you need to sleep. Another good way of getting some proper rest is to organize night shifts with your partner. You'll both have to wake up every few hours, so you should plan who will wake up and when. Ideally, shifts should be between six and seven hours long, so that one of you manages to get all the sleep they need while the other wakes up. Being able to take nights "off" to sleep consecutively is even better because you manage to recharge your batteries. In general, you should avoid the common mistake of staying awake all night together. You must ensure at least one of you gets proper rest during the night.

To avoid sleep deprivation, you must also find a routine and go to bed early. After your child falls asleep at night, you might be tempted to stay awake a bit longer and finally watch a TV series or movie on Netflix. As relaxing as it might look, you must go to bed as soon as you can because you don't know what will happen next. Your baby might wake up after a few hours just as you've finished watching TV and are ready to go to bed. Moreover, you must create a bedtime routine to fall asleep more easily and faster. I wouldn't recommend using screens before going to bed because they don't help you fall asleep. Alternatively, you can read a book, take a long and hot bath or shower, or light candles and turn the lights off. If you want, you can create a bedtime routine just with your partner or include your baby, too. For instance, you can all take a bath together to relax and deepen the emotional bond between the three of you.

Addressing Fears and Anxieties of Parenting

During pregnancy and after your baby's arrival, you might have mixed feelings. You might feel delighted in some moments and overwhelmed in others. You must accept that all emotions are essential to survive and are normal. Becoming a father is a huge step and change in your life, so you have every right to feel anxious and worried. If you want to properly handle your fears and anxieties, you must first accept that emotions are normal, and that you can't live without them—even if they're challenging. Sleep deprivation doesn't help you feel better, as it might make you feel more irritated and exhausted than usual. Consequently, negative emotions might keep increasing. At the same time, you might struggle to find some free time or time you can't dedicate to your significant other. Therefore, you might convince yourself you're ruining your relationship and can't have a minute for yourself. Such situations can also boost negative emotions and make you feel overwhelmed.

You might also feel lonely and isolated because you feel like nobody can understand what you're going through, not even other fathers or friends who also have babies. You might also feel disconnected from your previous life when your partner wasn't pregnant, or you didn't have a baby, or you might feel consumed with doing nothing except caring for your child. You might feel anxious also because you don't know what will happen next; you're afraid you'll fail as a father, you're worried about providing for your family, or you're afraid you'll never bond with your child. In other words, your biggest fears concern your relationship with your loved one and baby and how you'll deal with becoming a father.

Whenever you feel like you're doomed and will never be a good father, remember that you're not alone. Many other fathers around the world share the same concerns, worries, and doubts. We all fear not being perfect or at least good enough for our babies. We all want to do more to raise them properly and be there for them. However, we're just human beings, so we can't expect to be perfect and excel at everything we do. Even as fathers, we'll make mistakes, so try to learn from them. That's the best thing we can do. To increase your mood and reduce stress and anxiety, you can try to repeat to yourself that you're a great father and you're doing an incredible job raising your child. You mustn't only tell it to yourself but also believe in it because it's true. Don't be too hard on yourself; appreciate all the good things you're doing for your child.

Moreover, keep in mind your partner will always support you. If you have doubts or feel negative emotions, you can discuss them. I'm sure they'll appreciate you opening up to them and will carefully listen to what you want to tell them. You're a team that must work together to succeed. If you close yourself off, your relationship might be affected by your behavior. Whenever you feel blue and believe you're not getting better as a father, ask for feedback. They'll probably highlight the small things you do every day to take care of them and your baby that you weren't even aware of. Consequently, you'll realize you're doing much more than you believe.

In addition to asking for help, you must also take care of yourself. Even if you don't have time to do anything, think about when you might have a few minutes to dedicate to yourself. It can be eating something you enjoy, taking a short walk outside, putting on your earphones and listening to music, and so on. You can't even imagine all the ways you can relax and lighten up your moods in just a few minutes. You can tell a joke to your partner and laugh together or have an interesting conversation on a topic that is different from taking care of your child.

To take care of yourself and reduce fears and anxiety, you might also need professional help. You shouldn't feel ashamed or embarrassed if you decide to start therapy with a psychologist or other expert. Conversely, they can help you face your fears and live a happy life. A therapist guides you through the reasons behind your fears and anxieties, changing the perception you have of them, and setting realistic expectations for your future. Asking for a therapist's help only has positive effects. Not only can they help you become aware of yourself, but they also improve your relationship with your partner and baby.

Creating a Support System: Finding Dad Groups and Communities

As you've just learned, your understandable fears and anxieties linked with fatherhood might hinder your relationships with others and your child and reduce your mental and physical health. For these reasons, you must take care of yourself and ask for help from others. In addition to turning to your partner or a therapist, you can create a support system with other fathers. At the end of Chapter 1, you discovered the importance of a community that supports you and encourages you to do your best as a father. Now, we'll take a closer look at why and how you can ask for other fathers' help.

Sharing your struggles and worries with other fathers helps you understand you're not the only one experiencing this, and others can understand and advise you. Moreover, you might find it hard to receive help from other family members or professionals, like doctors and nurses. In fact, society is still struggling to understand that fathers are just as nurturing and engaged as mothers. Therefore, doctors and nurses might not provide adequate help for dads who are looking for someone to answer their questions and make them feel better. In most cases, they focus on the mother and consider the father as someone who can help and not an active and involved family member. That's why you might need to vent and discuss your emotions with someone who listens to you: other fathers in the same situation. Consulting with other dads can help you deal with your fears and anxiety. You discover the next steps you must take as a father and that you're not as bad as you think. Talking to other fathers can show you everybody makes mistakes and try to fix them in the best way they can. Moreover, other dads can give you some useful tips and advice on how to maintain a good relationship with your partner.

How can you ask for other fathers' help? You can find a group of local dads that regularly gather together to discuss and tackle issues and worries linked with fatherhood. You can probably find a dad group nearby just by searching for the city where you live (or a close and bigger city) and the respective dad group. If you can't find one close to you, you can also start your own. If you struggle with discussing your problems face-to-face, you can join one of the many dad group communities and forums to ask for advice, vent, or share your daily accomplishments. Remember, nobody will judge you for your situation, as you'll find many single or divorced dads, as well as experienced fathers and other first-time dads, just like you.

To find offline support groups, just ask around. Talk to other dads you know or look around your city to see if you notice some flyers or posters that talk about fathers helping each other. Alternatively, you can look on social media platforms, like Facebook or Instagram, where such groups might organize to meet in person. To find online support, you must search for the best support group for you. If you don't know where to start, you can try Fathers4Kids, The Fathers' Rights Movement, National Fatherhood Initiative, MensGroup, and Natural Resources Dads Group. Fathers4Kids aims to help fathers become aware of all the legal opportunities they have to dedicate more time to their children, like taking parental leave or getting visitation rights. The Fathers' Rights Movement provides information for fathers wanting to know everything about childcare, national laws, etc. National Fatherhood Initiative allows you to become a 24/7 father who properly dedicates yourself to their child and successfully balances work and life. MensGroup offers you the opportunity to openly and comfortably discuss all sorts of issues and worries you have. Finally, Natural Resources Dads Group tackles questions and doubts linked to fatherhood, like parenting strategies, supporting your partner, and taking care of yourself.

Interactive Element

You might look forward to becoming more aware of your emotions, fears, and anxieties, but don't know where to start. If you're not used to sharing your inner self with people, you might need to practice first. That's why you'll find some useful journal prompts below. You can use them to keep your journal and write down your thoughts and feelings or to practice sharing what you have inside. This way, it'll become easier when you discuss with other fathers or a therapist. Write down the answers and reflect on the following sentences.

- Write down three things you're grateful for as a dad.
- What are some of the biggest challenges you have faced as a dad, and how have you dealt with them?
- How do you want your children to describe you when they are older?
- Write down five things you're proud of as a dad.
- What are some of the things that make you feel closer to your children?
- Do you regret some choices you made as a father? How would you change them?
- What are your goals as a father?
- How do you show love to your baby?
- Write down five things you've learned from your child.
- How do you take care of your mental and physical health?
- How can you improve communication with your baby?
- What are some of the things that stress you out as a dad, and how do you manage those stressors?

In this chapter, we discussed the most common problems, fears, and anxieties of a father. We discovered sleep deprivation is inevitable, but we must do something about it if we don't want to hinder our mental and physical health and our relationship with others and our children. Therefore, we must take care of ourselves and take advantage of all occasions to get some sleep. We must also organize night shifts with our partners and collaborate with them. Some common fears and anxieties include the fear of not being a good father, not knowing what will happen next, being alone, and not dedicating enough time to ourselves. To overcome such fears, we must take a few minutes daily to do something we enjoy and discuss with our partners or a professional. We can also look for other fathers' help offline or online. Finally, we looked at some useful prompts that can help us reflect on our emotions and fears. As you master the art of navigating the challenges of new fatherhood, you'll find that it paves the way to forming unbreakable bonds with your child. Let's journey into the heart of these connections in our next chapter.

7

Nurturing Lasting Connections With Your Child

Children will not remember you for the material things you provided but for the feeling that you cherished them.

Richard L. Evans

The moments we share with our children aren't just about passing time—they're about making every second count. These are the memories that shape who they become and the bond that lasts a lifetime. To create a lasting connection with our babies, we must give significance to every minute we spend with them. When they grow up, they won't remember if you bought them one or three ice creams per month but how you made them feel. If they laughed with you, learned from you, and discovered incredible things thanks to you, then they'll build a strong and deep relationship with you. In this chapter, you'll learn all the ingredients you need to make sure you develop a long-lasting connection with your baby. You'll discover the significance of routine and prioritizing quality time over quantity. You'll also learn all the roles you can have in the relationship with your baby and how to encourage a love of learning and exploration. Finally, you'll look at a practical activity to help you keep track of all the things you try with your child.

The Centrality of Routine in Bonding

It's commonly understood that routines help our children's development, but do you know why exactly? Just think about your life and how you feel when you know what will happen next. If you're used to scheduling your tasks and planning your activities, you might feel relaxed and happy. Predictability is essential for human beings' survival and well-being, so you can imagine it's paramount for our children. Thanks to a well-established routine, your child feels secure, safe, and comfortable. They feel like they're in control of the environment and enjoy each activity they practice because they're aware of how much it will last and what will occur after that. They're also more likely to focus on learning and feel more engaged. Studies have found that children with a routine are more likely to develop healthy social and emotional skills, especially self-regulation skills (Bocknek, 2020). If they know how to regulate their emotions and reactions, they can better adapt to new environments and situations. They're also more likely to make new friends and build positive relationships. As with all other skills, self-regulation requires time and effort. The more you create a secure and comfortable environment, the more likely your child will develop a healthy routine and learn to regulate emotions.

How can you develop a routine with your child? You must start now by continuing to do the activities you're already doing. If you've been with your partner for a long time, you might already have established some essential routines, like getting together to cook and have dinner or watching a TV series before going to bed. You can do the same activities with your baby. Ensure your daily life is predictable and involve your child in your routine. Obviously, you must choose age-appropriate tasks, like avoiding horror movies with them or making them cook dinner with you when they're very little. When they're just born and not able to do much on their own, you can focus on playing with them. Just a few minutes every day is enough to make them happy, although you must show consistency. If you know you must work until 6 p.m., try to find some time when you get home to dedicate to your child. Remember not to force routines on them because they realize when something's off, even if they're very little. You must find the perfect routine without distorting your daily life and forcing yourself to do specific activities at the same time. If you can't comply with your routine, you might feel stressed or frustrated, thus risking making your child feel anxious, too.

Dive Into Story Time, Playtime, and Quality Time

In Chapter 3, we analyzed various ways in which you can develop a deep emotional bond with your child. You discovered playing, talking, and staying physically close to them to boost your connection. However, we didn't delve into story time, playtime, and quality time. When discussing the importance of talking to your baby, we briefly discovered how reading and singing to them can foster their development. In fact, research has found that reading books and telling stories promotes imagination, brain development, language, and learning (Nedovic, 2018). The earlier you start reading or singing to your child, the more easily they'll develop the above essential life skills. When you read or tell a story, your child recognizes and understands sounds and words that will come in handy when they grow up. They'll develop good communication skills, concentrate better, and learn new amazing things about the world around them. Reading stories boosts their imagination and curiosity and sparks their interest in learning. You can easily integrate reading into your daily routine by reading or singing to your child before going to bed, for example. Remember, most of the time, especially when they're very little, you don't need to read a whole book in one night. You can just hug or hold your baby while you keep a book in your hands and let them look at the pictures. You can comment on the pictures to foster their imagination and curiosity.

In addition to reading and telling stories to your baby, you must also play with them. Play fosters all aspects of their development, so you must dedicate as much time as you can to it (*Why*

Play Is Important, 2019). Playing helps children develop self-confidence and feel loved, safe, and happy. It also allows them to understand how the world works and develop physical and social skills. When children play, they learn to interact with others and understand how their actions might positively or negatively impact their peers. Therefore, playing helps your baby communicate with and care for others. Moreover, play must often vary to foster your baby's development. They must learn to play indoors and outdoors, in groups or alone, and so on (*Why Play Is Important*, 2019). There are mainly two types of play: structured and unstructured. Structured play consists of organized playtime led by a grown-up at a fixed time or space, like dance classes, board games, or outdoor ball games. Unstructured play is also called free play and consists of letting your child play as they want. The only role you can have in unstructured play is guiding them in the right direction or encouraging them by asking questions and clarifying what they're doing. With your newborn baby, you can just sing with them, tickle them, play peek-a-boo, or show them objects of different sizes and shapes.

Quality time is different from quantity time, but the former can foster the latter. If you start spending quality time with your baby, you can begin with just a few minutes every day. After some time, your baby and you will find so much joy and excitement in spending quality time together that you end up doing it more and more. Finally, your time together won't only be high quality but also increase in quantity. To spend more quality time with your child, completely focus on them when you spend time together, and avoid getting distracted by other people or devices. Read or tell a story and play with them. Make sure your baby understands they're the most important thing to you during those moments together. Sitting close to your baby on the couch and looking at your smartphone while they play a game on their iPad is not quality time. Watching their favorite cartoon or looking at an interesting object together is quality time because you are sharing something. When your baby finally arrives in your life, make sure to always prioritize quality over quantity. This way, you'll surely develop a deep and strong bond with them.

Roles in Relationship Building

Everyone can father a child, but being a father is much more complicated. In fact, dads play various roles in their children's lives and can't be replaced by anybody else in the world—not even mothers.

First of all, fathers foster their baby's emotional development, just like mothers do. Children look to their parents as role models who help them understand how to behave and how the world works. In particular, fathers foster self-confidence and security in them. If fathers are predictable, supportive, and affectionate, then their babies will feel secure, protected, and confident. Research has shown that fathers' love and support have a huge positive impact on their children's cognitive and social development (*The Importance of a Father in a Child's Life*, 2018). In general, children want to make their fathers proud, so they'll always try to get their attention and show them what they can do. For these reasons, you must pay attention to what they do and say. When your baby can't talk or walk yet, even a simple sound or cry might indicate they're looking for you and want your attention. Fathers also help their children understand how to interact with others. In other words, your baby looks to you to learn how to behave in front of other people. In particular, the way you treat your child will have a long-lasting effect on how they will relate to their future friends, schoolmates, and partners, and how they'll choose them. If you try to be as honest as you can with your baby, they'll probably do the same in future relationships.

Depending on the gender of your baby, you might have a different influence on them. If you have a little girl, she will likely depend on you to develop emotionally and feel secure (*The Importance of a Father in a Child's Life*, 2018). If you have a deep and strong connection with her, she's more likely to look for positive relationships, especially with future partners. The healthier the relationship with you, the healthier relationships she will have as a teenager and adult. She will probably look for your qualities in other boys and men, so make sure to show her the best of yourself. If you have a boy, he's more likely to shape his identity and character after your personality. From a very young age, boys look for their father's approval, so pay attention to the actions and thoughts you reward. If you care and treat others respectfully, your boy will probably grow up the same. If you're absent or barely involved, your child is likely to look for approval from their peers or other figures that they consider important (*The Importance of a Father in a Child's Life*, 2018). Just keep in mind that not all children are the same. Although the above information might help you deal with your baby, your behavior might influence your child in various ways that you can't predict for sure.

Championing Early Learning and Exploration

Let's imagine you're in a waiting room and don't have your phone with you. What do you do? Alternatively, imagine driving your car, stopping at the traffic light, and noticing something weird crossing the street. Do you get out of your vehicle to check what it is or keep driving? If you don't know what to do in a waiting room and keep driving, then you might have lost some of the curiosity that accompanied you since you were born. Being curious is the essential element to spark interest in learning and understanding new things. The more your child is curious, the more they'll explore on their own and become satisfied adults. Children are naturally inquisitive, but they might lose such a quality over the years if you don't help them develop it. When your baby finally arrives, you'll probably notice they feel like touching or even mouthing every object they see. If the item isn't dangerous for them, I suggest you let them do it because that's their way of doing their first explorations on their own. When they can't walk or run, they try to touch all the objects they can easily reach, like your necklace or bracelet.

What can you do to foster your child's curiosity from the first day of their life? First of all, you must encourage their interests, which will probably be objects when they're very little. Hold them while showing them the house, and stop when they point at something with their little fingers. If it's not dangerous, get close and let them touch it. Even if they can't understand you, talk to them with a high-pitched voice, describe the object, and tell a story about it, like when and where you bought it. Your baby will be amazed by your words and curious to know more. If you want, you can also give objects to them and see how they react. If they're not particularly interested, you can try another item. A common mistake many parents make is to just say "No" or "Don't" to their children. If you notice they like doing something that bothers you or might dirty the house, think about a solution to let them play without causing too much trouble. For instance, you can dedicate a specific spot in the house to playtime and let your baby do what they want. In general, your baby will see you as an example and role model to follow. If you show them you're curious, ask a lot of questions, and look for answers to understand the world, they'll be more likely to do the same as adults.

Once your baby finally manages to talk, you might find yourself in a difficult situation. In fact, they might keep asking you questions, especially "Why?" This is a fundamental stage of your child's development as they show interest and curiosity for what happens around them. Many parents might get annoyed by the infinite number of questions and just answer "I don't know" or divert their children's attention to something different. However, the most effective way of boosting your child's curiosity is to let them ask and answer in the best possible way. If you truly don't know how to reply, just be honest and look for an appropriate answer together with your child. Remember, they will never stop learning from you and see you as a role model. As they grow up, keep practicing the healthy and positive habits and routines you established during the first months and years of their life. Just make sure to adapt to the various stages and behave accordingly.

Interactive Element

At this point, you might be wondering how you can keep track of all the activities you want to try with your newborn baby. To build a strong and deep emotional bond, you might want to complete various tasks in your daily life. For this reason, you might need a checklist to mark down all the different activities you do together. You can use the following checklist as a starting point to create your own and add all the things you want to try. Mark with an "X" the activities you do every day with your child. After using the checklist for a week, reflect on the tasks you do the most and the ones you neglect. Then, adjust your routine to include as many activities as you can and try different ones.

Activity	Mon	Tue	Wed	Thu	Fri	Sat	Sun
Cuddling							
Peek-a-boo							
Singing a song							
Telling a story							
Reading							
Exploring							
Talking							
Free play							
Tickling							

In this chapter, we dove deep into the topic of creating an emotional and long-lasting bond with our children. We discovered routine is essential to make our babies feel secure, comfortable, and confident enough to explore the environment independently and learn. Next, we discussed the importance of spending quality time together by playing, reading, or telling stories to our children. We also looked at all the various roles we play as fathers in our babies' development. Thanks to us, they develop emotional and social skills and learn how to interact with others. Then, we discovered ways in which we can foster curiosity and a love of learning in our babies, which are fundamental skills they will need in the future. Finally, we looked at a useful checklist that helps us keep track of all the daily activities we practice with our children. As we take the journey of bonding and connecting, we must remember the key isn't just about being there, but truly being present. We'll dive deep into the topic of being present and fostering positive parenting in the next chapter.

8

Being Present—The Key to Positive Parenting

Being present for your child has incredible effects on their mental and physical health and their future in general. Did you know that children who have an actively involved father are 33% less likely to repeat a grade at school and 43% more likely to get A's (*A Father's Impact on Child Development,* 2018)? This is just an example of the positive impact an involved father has on their child's life. Thanks to this chapter, you'll discover the profound influence of being present and will be equipped with actionable techniques to stay focused even amid parenting chaos. In particular, this chapter will teach you the importance of mindfulness and how to practice it in your daily life. Next, it will show you other useful techniques to stay present in challenging situations. Then, it will highlight the long-term benefits of being an engaged father. Finally, there will be an interactive element to help you stay positive and appreciate your life.

The Importance of Mindfulness in Fatherhood

Becoming a father is rewarding and fulfilling, just as it is challenging and stressful. You must put all your effort and energy into raising your child, which can be hard sometimes. For this reason, you might need to practice a technique that helps you stay focused. Mindfulness is an ancient practice that allows people to stay in the here and now. Thanks to mindfulness, you can fully live every moment of your life. You just focus on what's happening right now and don't think about past or future events. When you're mindful, you slow down and hit the pause button on your worries and anxieties. Try to think about the last time you were fully focused on an activity or conversation with someone. Can you remember it? If not, you don't have to worry, as it's quite common. Most people tend to think about past or future events while completing daily tasks or talking to others. However, that's not the best way to live your life, especially if you're a father and want to do your best to raise your child.

Mindfulness allows you to focus on your thoughts, emotions, and physical sensations without judging them. Thanks to this practice, you learn to appreciate every moment and accept everything that happens—good or bad. You discover how to live your life while reducing or keeping your worries under control. Mindfulness practices mainly involve meditation, but it doesn't mean you must spend hours sitting with your eyes closed and focusing on your thoughts. Mindfulness is much easier than you might believe. In fact, you can practice it wherever and whenever you want, even for a few seconds or minutes.

How can mindfulness help you become a better father? Mindfulness boosts your overall well-being by reducing stress and anxiety. If you learn to stop focusing on the past or future, you focus on the present, thus reducing all your worries. If you accept things as they are, you also decrease the stress you might feel in forcing change in your life. Mindfulness helps you understand that worrying and concentrating on negative thoughts won't help you solve your problems. Conversely, staying positive and living in the present will. Consequently, mindfulness allows you to accept change and face challenges with the right attitude. As you might guess, the main benefit of this practice is that it increases your focus and concentration on your daily activities. It also boosts your empathy and under-standing and helps you make better decisions. If you're mind-ful, you create a deep bond with your baby and understand their needs. You also know what's best for them and consider your partner's opinion. Therefore, you try to find solutions that can benefit all of you. As you can see, mindfulness can have positive effects on your relationship.

To practice mindfulness, you must pay attention to your feelings and thoughts. Whenever you're together with your child, ask yourself how you feel. Try to label and understand all the emotions you feel—negative and positive. Reflect on your reac-tions when you do something with your baby, especially if you feel like you're about to react with anger. Take a few seconds or minutes, think about your emotional reaction, and consider alternative ways in which you can respond. In order to do so, you must learn to practice mindful breathing, which consists of taking long, deep breaths. If you want, you can close your eyes to make the exercise easier to practice. Focus on the air you breathe in and out, and notice the physical sensations you feel, especially in your belly. To master the technique, I suggest you first try it in a quiet environment when you feel relaxed. Take slow and deep breaths for a few seconds or a minute, and then keep doing your daily activities. After some time, you can practice mindful breathing in stressful situations and for more than a minute. The real secret to properly mastering mindfulness is to focus all your attention on one activity or person. If your baby smiles at you, focus on their facial expression and gesture, and nothing else. If you're playing with them, avoid thinking about your job or what you have to do next. Just enjoy every moment you spend with your child, even if it's just looking at them or laughing together.

Techniques to Stay Present Amidst Chaos

Being mindful is not the only way to stay present in the moment and focus on your child. You can practice various tips and techniques to pay attention to your actions. For example, you should put your phone away when you're with your little one. You might think you can look at social media when you have some free time with your child, so you prefer to keep your phone near you. Alternatively, you might wait for an urgent call from work, so you bring your phone with you around the house. You must always remember to prioritize your baby. You can scroll social media or answer the urgent call after you've put them in bed. In addition to putting your phone away, you must also avoid the temptation to put a screen in front of your baby when they feel distressed or frustrated. This is an unhealthy habit that might lead them to spend too much time on their phones when they become teenagers and adults. Keep in mind you're your baby's first role model. If you spend quality time with them and put away all the screens that might distract you, you're more likely to build a long-lasting bond and pass down healthy habits to them.

Another effective technique to be present with your child is to dedicate at least a few minutes every day to having fun. It doesn't mean you must play with them, but do something crazy. Sing a song you like even if you think you're not in tune or run around the house with your child. Obviously, you must choose age-appropriate tasks. With your newborn baby, you can make silly faces in front of them, show your tongue, or use weird voices. You can try to imitate the voice of a famous cartoon character or something similar. Alternatively, you can show your baby your dancing skills and move in front of them. Just go crazy and enjoy all the moments with your child. You can integrate those "go wild" moments into your daily routine and try to repeat them over the years. When your child becomes older, you can still do crazy things with them.

To stay present, you must also learn to be grateful for what you have. Too many times, people focus on all the negative things that happen to them and forget about the positive ones. Have you ever thought your life was a mess, even if it wasn't that bad? I'm sure you have. Whenever you feel like your world's falling apart and you're doomed to fail, stop for a few seconds or minutes, and focus on the good things around you. You'll discover you have loved ones who always support you, your baby is beautiful, and your job is much better than many others. In other words, perceive your life as a gift. Be thankful for all the positive events and people around you. Instead of complaining to your partner because they didn't listen to you once, thank them for being there for you. When you think of negative aspects, analyze your thoughts, and ask yourself if they match reality. In most cases, your thoughts are a distorted vision of what happens around you.

Finally, a good way of being present is to think that you won't always be with your child. Your baby will grow much faster than you think, and before you know it, they're able to go to school by themselves, go out with their friends, and much more. Enjoy all the moments with your baby right now, as they won't last. When they grow up, they'll live their own lives, probably away from you. Even before becoming independent, they'll start going to school, thus spending more time outside the house. Take advantage of every single minute you live with them and fully enjoy all the moments together.

As you already learned, being organized is essential to managing your life and finding the perfect work-life balance. Planning your activities is also important to being present with your child. Schedule your time with them, possible distractions, and duties. For instance, you can schedule spending 10 minutes every day after work to play or go wild with your baby. When they go to bed, you can schedule half an hour to scroll social media and watch the news. This way, you'll always know you have time dedicated to your child and be present.

The Long-Term Benefits of Being an Engaged Dad

At the beginning of this chapter, we looked at research that shows how fathers' involvement increases their children's school performance. Now, we'll dive deep into the benefits that engagement can have on your baby's life. First of all, what does "being engaged" mean as a father? An involved dad is both physically and emotionally present and provides support on different occasions (*Why Fatherhood Engagement Matters*, 2017). An engaged father also shows genuine interest in their child's activities, emotions, thoughts, and behavior. In other words, they listen and try to understand their children's needs and wants and are actively involved in their daily activities, like homework or hobbies.

The earlier you start being present in your baby's life, the more positive effects you'll see in the short and long term. Studies have found that fathers' engagement is just as important as mothers' (*Why Fatherhood Engagement Matters*, 2017). Children with an involved dad are more likely to grow healthy because they improve the rate at which they gain weight if they were born preterm and increase their breastfeeding rates. Conversely, babies with uninvolved fathers are more at risk of developing psychological disorders. Fathers' involvement also has different effects depending on their children's gender. Research has shown that involved fathers reduce boys' risk of developing behavioral problems and girls' risk of developing mental health disorders (*Why Fatherhood Engagement Matters*, 2017).

In general, children with involved fathers are more likely to build strong and deep relationships as adults and have better chances for success (*Why Fatherhood Engagement Matters*, 2017). They're more likely to have a long-lasting marriage and feel satisfied with their relationships with their significant others, friends, and coworkers. Engaged dads provide emotional support that helps children understand others' emotions and how to behave. In other words, they develop essential life skills, such as self-confidence.

Moreover, children with engaged fathers are more likely to perform better at school and find stable employment. When your baby starts going to school, you must talk to teachers, ask them questions about what they did during the day with your child, and get to know other parents and children. This way, your child will learn better and faster and engage in healthier classroom behavior. Even when they become adults, they'll be more likely to find a satisfying and stable job and less likely to spend time in jail or have a baby on their own during their teenage years. Being engaged as soon as your child goes to kindergarten has a ripple effect on their future success (*Why Fatherhood Engagement Matters*, 2017).

Being present with your baby also increases the probability of them being happy and feeling satisfied (*Why Fatherhood Engagement Matters*, 2017). Studies have found that the father's presence encourages babies to explore the environment around them by themselves and feel confident. Therefore, they're not afraid to try new things without their parents' help. As adults, they're more likely to become autonomous and independent, which leads to a satisfying life. Your child will be able to make good decisions independently and understand what's best for them. They won't need anybody's approval to do what they want and like and pursue their goals. Having an involved father also helps children properly handle stress as adults.

Being an involved dad doesn't only have positive effects on your child but on yourself, too. Looking at them succeeding and having a happy life is already enough to make you feel better. But being present also means building a positive relationship with your child, growing as an individual, and making better decisions. As you can see, your presence as a father can only make your baby's and your life happier.

Interactive Element

In the previous chapters, we looked at practical activities you can do to analyze your emotions and thoughts, especially negative ones. Now, it's time to be positive. The following activity is simple: You just have to repeat to yourself the positive affirmations you'll find below every day. Focus on the bright side, empower yourself to face every challenge, and feel satisfied at the end of each day. Sometimes, looking at the good things in your life might be difficult, and that's why you might need some help in letting go of negative thoughts. Positive affirmations are also a typical exercise of mindfulness that helps you focus on your strengths and be thankful for what you have. Read the following affirmations and repeat them to yourself daily, or write them down somewhere you can easily spot them. If you want, you can also use Post-its and scatter all those positive affirmations around the house.

- I trust my instincts as a father and partner.
- I am confident.
- My partner recognizes and respects my efforts.
- My family values me.
- I have a lot to offer my family.
- I deserve to be loved.
- I support others as they support me.
- I give my best self.
- I choose love over fear.
- I am ready to be a father to this child.
- My life is increasing in joy.
- I can do hard things.
- My family is safer when I am present.
- The love in my family deepens when I help.
- I'm grateful for what I have.
- My partner and baby are safe.
- I can get through anything.
- If I get overwhelmed, I take a deep breath and release it.
- I believe in myself and my skills.
- I am strong and resilient.
- I can handle this situation.
- I am enough.
- This is my birth experience too.
- There is time and space for me to take care of myself.
- I value my child's, my partner's, and my own needs.

In this chapter, we focused on the importance of being involved. We discovered that our presence as fathers from the day our child is born has long-lasting effects on their mental and physical health, and ensures our baby's success. We also learned useful and easy techniques we can practice every day to be present. Thanks to mindfulness, we can focus on our child and nothing else. We can eliminate distractions and negative thoughts by taking long and deep breaths and paying attention to the things we are doing as we do them. Then, we found other techniques, like putting our phones away when we're with our children, having fun together, being grateful for what we have, and remembering our babies won't be close to us forever. Therefore, we must take advantage of every moment we spend with them. At this point, we have all the information we need to face the first few months and years of our baby's life. Now, it's time to glance ahead. In the next chapter, we'll discover how we can prepare for the future, ensuring our children have the foundation they need for a bright tomorrow.

9

Preparing for the Future

Between the time your baby is born and the day they turn 18, you'll have spent 6,570 days with them, 940 of those being Saturdays (Dell'Antonia, 2012). What do you plan to do during that time? It might sound scary and make you feel anxious thinking about the time you'll spend with your baby right now when you're still waiting for them, or they've just arrived in your life. However, as this book has shown you, it's always better to be prepared. When your child is born, days might look long or even infinite. You might feel like you don't have the time to do anything and wish days were 30 or even 40 hours long. After a few years, you'll look back at what you've done and be surprised by how fast time has passed. For this reason, you must reflect on how you would like to spend time with your baby. You must also prepare to face more challenging times when they grow up, become teenagers, and attend college. Thanks to this chapter, you'll be prepared for all of this.

You'll learn how to create family traditions and lasting memories to build a strong and deep bond with your child. You'll also discover the importance of financial planning and how to prepare for future expenses, like college. Next, you'll learn how your child's needs might change over the years and how to adapt. Finally, you'll look at a practical activity that shows you how to manage your finances.

Creating Family Traditions and Lasting Memories

As you learned in Chapter 7, babies love routine and consistency because they make them feel confident, secure, and protected. Consequently, they also enjoy family traditions, which consist of repeating the same activities every week, month, or year. Do you remember some family traditions you had as a child? Maybe you were used to waiting until the 25th of December to open all your gifts, painting eggs for Easter, or visiting relatives who lived far away from you during the holidays. These are examples of annual traditions, but you probably also had monthly and weekly ones, like Taco Day or a Sunday hike with your parents. When recalling your family traditions, do you feel nostalgic? I would imagine so, as they probably made you feel happy, and you looked forward to them.

Wouldn't you want to create similar or completely new family traditions with your newborn baby? If so, you don't have to do much. You can keep repeating the activities you enjoy with your partner and include your baby. Obviously, you must always consider their age and what they can do. If you're used to preparing Christmas dinner with your partner starting in the morning, you can keep your baby close and show them how you do it. You can let them look at the tools and ingredients you handle and use a high-pitched tone of voice to spark their interest. If you enjoy walking around the neighborhood at the end of each day, you can include your child by taking them with you. As your baby grows, you adapt to the change. When they turn 7 or 8, you can let them help you cook and handle ingredients. You can also take longer walks or go to a park instead of staying around the neighborhood.

Why are traditions important for your child? In addition to making your baby feel confident and secure, they also provide a sense of identity, build character, and strengthen family bonds. Your traditions might be linked with your religion, culture, or just fun, but they always remind you where you come from and your values. In other words, traditions shape your family. Consequently, they allow your child to understand what you value in your life and where they come from. If you read a book to them daily, they'll know there's always time to learn. Such knowledge has a positive influence on their overall well-being and quality of life. Researchers have analyzed the impact that knowing about family traditions and history has had on children (Homes, n.d.). They discovered that the more children knew, the more positive feelings and essential skills they developed. In particular, they had higher self-esteem, felt more in control of their lives, and believed their family functioned properly. They were also more resilient and able to manage stress effectively. Family traditions also strengthen bonds because members learn to trust each other. They know that a specific day or moment will be dedicated only to the family and will be repeated every week, month, or year (Homes, n.d.).

Do you feel like changing your traditions or adding new ones that might be more suitable for a baby? Well, you have plenty of activities to choose from. For example, you can go on an annual vacation together, plan a weekly game night, invent, and use secret signals, or go camping. Alternatively, you can create traditions around the classical family holidays, like Christmas and Easter, or establish a birthday ritual. In general, you can start a new tradition linked with days, seasons, and festivities. You can repeat an activity every Saturday or Sunday, every summer or fall, every Thanksgiving or New Year's Day.

Financial Planning and Future Considerations for Your Growing Family

You surely want the best for your baby, so you might have already started organizing their room, buying essential items, and planning the future. A fundamental element each parent must consider is expenses. Until now, there were only two of you, so you probably didn't need a lot of financial planning. You probably went out for dinner when you could and didn't go out when you couldn't. With your newborn baby, you must think long-term. You might want to start saving money for school and college and make sure your baby will always have some money available in case of an emergency. In other words, you might want to plan how you want to spend your money. Financial planning is paramount to save for the future and prepare for all events—even the most unexpected ones.

How can you develop a sound financial plan? First, you must determine your net worth by subtracting all expenses. You can check your bank account if you're used to paying with a credit card or keep track of your monthly expenses and subtract them from your salary. Make sure to include all assets and money you earn in one way or another. Once you know the money you have available every month, you can officially start your financial plan. You can build an emergency fund where you regularly deposit money, so you know you always have some available. Obviously, you mustn't use the emergency fund except for emergencies. Therefore, avoid the temptation of using it to go shopping or buy unnecessary items. Life and health insurance is also essential to grant financial stability to your family. Life insurance protects your partner and baby in case you die, while health insurance allows you to avoid prohibitive and unexpected medical expenses. If you want to save for your child's education, you can also find a financial plan that helps you save for everything your baby might need in the future, like primary or secondary education, college, marriage, or setting up a business.

To ensure you properly develop your financial plan, you must consider both short-term and long-term goals. Think about your needs and what your baby might need in the future. Then, devise a strategy to ensure you have enough money to continue your life and still save for emergencies and plans. Moreover, you must look for detailed and reliable information about the possible funds, investments, and savings you can make to start building a future for your baby.

If you don't feel comfortable creating a financial plan alone, you can always hire a financial advisor. Even if you know about and understand finances, hiring an advisor might still be the best choice for properly handling your money and making sure you save enough for your child's future. Finances are an intricate topic for most people, and you might need to dedicate a lot of time to managing them. At the same time, you might get anxious or stressed because you don't know what's best or don't understand how to effectively save money using different funds. In the end, you might end up struggling a lot and still not understand how you can save and invest as you want. An advisor can help you craft a personalized investment plan considering how much you spend and earn each month and if you effectively invest your money. An advisor is also able to identify all the opportunities you have to save more money, invest, and grow your assets. Finally, hiring an advisor saves you time, energy, and effort.

Charting Out Your Fatherhood Journey: From Infancy to Adolescence

Financial planning is just one of the tricky topics connected to becoming a father and having a baby. Another one concerns understanding and adapting to your child's needs as they grow. When they're very little, they need you to change their diapers and feed them. As they keep growing, their needs become more and more complicated.

From the day your baby's born until they turn 5, they're in the pre-literate and early literacy stage. They learn fundamental skills, like standing on their own, walking and running, understanding language, learning new words, and reading. These are considered the most essential years of your child's life in which your presence plays a fundamental role. The way you help them approach learning and interacting with others will shape the rest of their life. Therefore, they need you to be a role model and teach them how to move around the world, but also to give them some freedom to explore on their own (*Meet Children's Needs as They Change Over Time*, 2023).

Between 6 and 9 years old, your child will attend elementary school, where they learn more complicated subjects, like math and science. At this age, children are already able to understand "adult" problems and participate in the conversations. They need to feel included in all aspects of family life and treated as adults. You can give them more freedom to explore relationships with their peers and learn on their own (*Meet Children's Needs as They Change over Time*, 2023).

The years between 10 and 12 are considered a transition period when your child realizes they're not little anymore, but they're not a grown-up yet. This time might be characterized by confusion and experimentation of various behaviors—both healthy and unhealthy. Your child might test your limits to try to understand what they can and can't do. They need to feel independent but also to know you're there for them when they need a guide (*Meet Children's Needs as They Change Over Time*, 2023).

When your child turns 13, they enter adolescence or the teenage years. If you remember that time in your life, you might recall how difficult it was. You might have explored physical and emotional boundaries by hanging out with different people and trying new activities, which sometimes might have been dangerous. At this point, your child will be perfectly able to understand what's considered bad and good and how they should behave. However, it doesn't mean they'll follow the rules and listen to you. They won't need you to tell them they're wrong, or they're making a mistake, or they should live their life differently, or similar sentences. They need you to support them and answer their questions when they have doubts (*Meet Children's Needs as They Change Over Time*, 2023).

When your child finally turns 17 or 18, they're approaching adulthood. They finish high school and decide what to do next. They might immediately go to college, take a gap year, or start working. From now on, your role as a father will endure a drastic change. Your child might leave the house and rent a room or an apartment on their own. They might find a stable partner and explore new cities and countries. They just need to live their life, create their own routines and traditions, and start their own family. Take advantage of every moment you spend with them, as you learned to do throughout your child's life and accept them as they are. You might not be with them as often as you were used to or as you'd like, but you'll always be their father. Therefore, keep showing love and affection and supporting their decisions (*Meet Children's Needs as They Change Over Time*, 2023).

In this book, you learned some essential skills you must develop to raise your child properly and build your confidence as a father. The fundamental skill you must cultivate over the years is adaptability. You must keep in mind you'll never be able to anticipate all stressful events that might occur in the future. This means you might not be prepared to face some of the situations that you'll have to. For these reasons, you must learn to adapt to all kinds of events. First, you must practice flexible thinking, or the ability to see things from multiple perspectives. For example, the first reaction to your child telling a lie might be to get angry and punish them. However, it might not be the most effective way of handling such a situation. Instead, you can reflect on your child's behavior and consider possible reasons behind it. You can even discuss the issue with them. Every time you face a problem, try to consider various solutions. If you're flexible, you know how to properly solve different types of problems using your creativity.

To become more adaptable, you must also pause from time to time and think about the big picture. You might feel overwhelmed by daily struggles and forget about your main goal or long-term dreams. Whenever you realize something's wrong with your life, take some time to reflect on what you did until that moment and how you can improve. You might need time for yourself, dedicate more time to your partner, or take a day off work. Taking a break from a busy life is paramount to promoting a positive environment at home and helping your child develop healthily. Another tip to become more flexible consists of focusing on the positive aspects of your life and building a growth mindset, as you learned in Chapter 2. Finally, you must remember nobody has ever raised your child before, so there's no instruction manual to follow. You must be willing to learn on the job, accept your mistakes, and be aware that you'll help your child learn as much as they'll help you grow.

Being a father is a lifelong learning process that always teaches you something new and unexpected.

Interactive Element

Do you need some help starting your financial planning? You can use the worksheet below. Before using it, reflect on your short-term and long-term goals and how much money you would like to save for your child. Then, use the worksheet to become aware of your expenses, income, and the money you manage to save monthly. Finally, adjust your goals or find ways to save more to manage your finances properly.

Monthly income	Jan	Feb	Mar	Apr	May	June
Salary						
Assets						
Part-time job						
Other						
Total Monthly income						
Monthly expenses	Jan	Feb	Mar	Apr	May	June
House						
Shopping						
Grocery						
Free time						
Subscriptions (Netflix, Amazon)						
Health						
Self-care						
Transportation						
Others						
Total monthly expenses						

After completing the worksheet for the first time, compare the estimated and real monthly savings and use the results to craft your financial planning and decide what you can and want to save. You can use the following worksheet as a starting point.

Monthly savings	Estimated	Real
Emergency fund		
Investments		
College fund		
School fund		
Extracurricular activities or hobbies		
Allowance		
Daycare		
Others		
Total monthly savings		

In this chapter, we learned how to prepare for the future. We discovered the importance of traditions, how to create them, and some examples of family routines that we might try with our children. Next, we tackled the sensitive issue of finances by learning how we can craft our personal financial plans. We discovered we must become aware of our income and expenses to know how much money we can save, and we might need to hire a financial advisor if we want to save time and energy. Then, we briefly looked at how our children's needs might change over the years, and we learned how to develop adaptability, which is an essential skill for every parent. Finally, we looked at a useful worksheet to track our monthly income and expenses and calculate our savings. As we approach the book's conclusion, it's essential to take a moment to reflect.

Fatherhood is not just about navigating the early days or tackling daily challenges; it's about envisioning the future and setting the stage for a lifetime of memories, growth, and love. Let's recap the lessons and insights that have paved your journey to mastering the art of fatherhood.

Make a Difference with Your Dad Review

Unlock the Power of Fatherhood

"Being a dad isn't about being perfect. It's about being there."

Unknown

Hello there, Awesome Dads.

You just finished "First-Time Dad Mastery" by Dante A. Cacal. Wow, what a journey, right? Like the book says, maybe you spent months or years thinking about being a dad. Or maybe the news came as a big surprise! Either way, becoming a dad is like riding the biggest, wildest roller-coaster ever. Some days you feel super brave and ready. Other days, you might wonder, "Can I really do this?"

Becoming a father is a gift, an adventure, a challenge, and a joy. Our goal is to make this journey into fatherhood accessible to everyone. Your experiences, combined with the wisdom in this book, can become a beacon.

I humbly request your help. Be the guiding star for another dad out there. Most people do, in fact, judge a book by its cover (and its reviews). So, leave a review, share your story, and let's help another first-time dad out there.

To share the love, the laughs, and the lessons, all you need to do is...

Leave a review

Thank you from the bottom of my heart for being a part of this journey and for sharing the love. You're not just a great dad; you're also helping to build a community of awesome dads!

Simply scan the QR code or visit the link below to share your thoughts:

https://www.amazon.com/review/create-review/?
asin=B0CXGFF4JR

Conclusion

At this point, you have all the information and tools you need to face fatherhood with the right mindset. You left all your worries and doubts behind and are ready to face any challenge.

Chapter 1 provided a brief overview of how the role of fatherhood changed over the centuries and how it recently transformed. Like many other fathers, you look to be present in your child's life and help them develop physically and emotionally. You want to be there for your partner and participate as an active member in your family life. Chapter 1 also showed you the importance of culture and how to embrace cultural diversity with your partner. In Chapter 2, you learned how to cultivate positive thinking and a growth mindset to effectively face challenges and avoid negative feelings. You learned to accept change and take advantage of it to grow as an individual. You also discovered the importance of looking at the bright side even in the darkest hours.

Chapter 3 showed you some techniques to foster a deep emotional bond with your child, like kangaroo care or skin-to-skin contact, reading and talking to them, and playing peek-a-boo. All children need to be physically close to their parents, hear their voices, and have fun with them. In Chapter 4, you discovered how difficult it might be to balance work and life after your baby is born. That's why you must use time management techniques and set boundaries with your colleagues to dedicate enough time to your family.

In Chapter 5, you learned that you might feel mixed feelings once your baby is born. In particular, your relationships might change, and you might regret the day you decided to have a baby. You must accept those feelings because they're normal and try to keep a healthy and positive relationship with your significant other by working on your communication skills and understanding their physical and emotional changes during and after pregnancy. Chapter 6 focused on how to overcome the most common challenges of fatherhood, like sleep deprivation and common fears and anxieties. The key takeaway of the chapter is that you must always openly talk about your feelings with your partner and find a solution to your problems together. You can also turn to other fathers to receive feedback or advice.

In Chapter 7, you learned how routine makes your child feel secure and confident and how you must let them explore the world on their own in order to foster a love of learning and make them autonomous and independent adults. You also discovered quality is more important than quantity, so you must focus on how you spend your time with your baby rather than for how long. Even if it's just a few minutes every day, you must dedicate it to them. Chapter 8 discussed techniques in which you can be more present with your child, like mindfulness and avoiding distractions when interacting with your baby. You learned that being present can have long-lasting effects on your child's life, like enhancing academic performance, fostering success, and improving relationships with others. Finally, Chapter 9 focused on the future and showed you how to craft your financial plan to save money, how your child's needs might change over the years, and how to develop long-lasting traditions.

Are you ready to start the exciting journey of fatherhood? Take a moment today, right now, to think of one actionable step you can implement from this book in the coming week. Whether it's starting a new family tradition, setting up a financial plan, or simply spending an extra hour of quality time with your child—commit to it. Your future self and your child will thank you. If a chapter or lesson from this book resonated with you, share it with another dad or parent-to-be. After all, the journey of fatherhood is all the more enriching when shared with fellow travelers.

References

Adams, C. B. L. (2022, November 15). *Can fathers be maternal?* Psychology Today. https://www.psychologytoday.com/intl/blog/living-automatic/202211/can-fathers-be-maternal#:

All about skin-to-skin contact (kangaroo care). (2017). Pampers. https://www.pampers.com/en-us/pregnancy/giving-birth/article/skin-to-skin-contact

Antoine François Prévost d'Exiles quotes. (n.d.). Good Reads. https://www.goodreads.com/quotes/294893-the-heart-of-a-father-is-the-masterpiece-of-nature

As a new, first-time dad, I hate my baby intensely – what do I do? (2018). Reddit. https://www.reddit.com/r/AskParents/comments/aaqabm/as_a_new_firsttime_dad_i_hate_my_baby_intensely/

The best prioritization techniques in 2023. (2022, November 17). Timeular. https://timeular.com/blog/best-prioritization-techniques/

Best resources for new dads. (2022, November 16). Babylist. https://www.babylist.com/hello-baby/dad-groups

The best ways for new dads to bond with their baby. (n.d.). Emma's Diary. https://www.emmasdiary.co.uk/baby/new-born-care/dad-bonding-advice

Bocknek, E. (2020, April 1). *The importance of routines for kids.* Zero to Thrive. https://zerotothrive.org/routines-for-kids/

Braswell, K. (2023, April 19). *The importance of mindfulness in fatherhood.* Dads Pad Blog. https://dadspadblog.com/2023/04/19/the-importance-of-mindfulness-in-fatherhood/

Canzater, S. L. (2019, July 11). *Talk to me, baby! The benefits of frequent, high-quality conversations with babies on brain and language development.* O'Neill Institute. https://oneill.law.georgetown.edu/talk-to-me-baby-the-benefits-of-frequent-high-quality-conversations-with-babies-on-brain-and-language-development/

The changing role of the modern day father. (2009). American Psychological Association. https://www.apa.org/pi/families/resources/changing-father

Check, B. (2019, September 10). *How fatherhood in America has changed over the years.* The Daily Dad. https://dailydad.com/how-fatherhood-has-changed-over-the-years/

Check, B. (2020, February 18). *How to be more present with your kids: Seven principles to keep in mind every day*. The Daily Dad. https://dailydad.com/be-more-present-with-your-kids/

Collier, E. (2019, May 24). *Why is reading so important for children?* High Speed Training. https://www.highspeedtraining.co.uk/hub/why-is-reading-important-for-children/

Curran, A. (2021, June 7). *Blending traditions: A Father's Day interview with TNJFON's newest dad*. TNJFON. https://www.tnjfon.org/blog/2021/6/7/blending-traditions-a-fathers-day-interview-with-tnjfons-newest-dad

Dad's role has changed over the years. (2019, August 19). Healthy Place. https://www.healthyplace.com/parenting/dads/dads-role-has-changed#:

Dell'Antonia, K. J. (2012, March 16). *Childhood: 940 Saturdays, and you're done*. The New York Times. https://archive.nytimes.com/parenting.blogs.nytimes.com/2012/03/16/childhood-940-saturdays-and-youre-done/

Dungy, T. (2015, February 19). *Why positive thinking is important*. All Pro Dad. https://www.allprodad.com/why-positive-thinking-is-important/

Dyson, B. (n.d.) In Mustering motivation (2015). *British Dental Journal, 218*(8), 442–443. https://doi.org/10.1038/sj.bdj.2015.309

Eng, J. (2021, November 15). *7 tricks for staying present in the moment as a parent*. ParentsTogether. https://parents-together.org/7-tricks-for-staying-present-in-the-moment-as-a-parent/

Evans, R. L. (n.d.). *Richard L. Evans Quotes*. Brainy Quote. https://www.brainyquote.com/quotes/richard_l_evans_135056

A father's impact on child development. (2018, June 7). Children's Bureau. https://www.all4kids.org/news/blog/a-fathers-impact-on-child-development/

Fathers: powerful allies for maternal and child health. (n.d.). National Institute for Children's Health Quality. https://nichq.org/insight/fathers-powerful-allies-maternal-and-child-health

Financial planning is a key feature of responsible parenthood. (n.d.). Ageas Federal. https://www.ageasfederal.com/blog/financial-planning-key-feature-responsible-parenthood

Find a Dad Group. (n.d.). The National At-Home Dad Network. https://athomedad.org/community/find-a-dad-group/

Five advantages of consulting with a financial advisor. (2022, October 11). Saddock Wealth. https://saddockwealth.com/five-advantages-of-consulting-with-a-financial-advisor/

Galla, S. (n.d.). *Father support groups - a guide to support groups for dads.* MensGroup. https://mensgroup.com/father-support-groups/

Geggel, L. (2018, August 12). *18 ways pregnancy may change your body forever.* Live Science. https://www.livescience.com/63291-post-pregnancy-changes.html

Grabmeier, J. (2020, March 17). *Babies may spark jealousy in partners with anxiety.* The Ohio State University. https://ehe.osu.edu/news/listing/babies-may-spark-jealousy-partners-anxiety

Haelle, T., & Willingham, E. (2019). *For new parents, dad may be the one missing the most sleep.* Npr. https://www.npr.org/sections/health-shots/2016/04/05/473002684/for-new-parents-dad-may-be-the-one-missing-the-most-sleep

Hakimi, A. P. (2023, March 20). *Workplace boundaries are way more important than you think!* Linkedin. https://www.linkedin.com/pulse/workplace-boundaries-way-more-important-than-you-adel/

Hall, T. (2019, June 14). *5 important ways fathers impact child development.* Child Care Resources. https://ccrnj.org/5-important-ways-fathers-impact-child-development/

Herrity, J. (2018). *11 active listening skills to practice (with examples).* Indeed. https://www.indeed.com/career-advice/career-development/active-listening-skills

Hold me close—physical touch and brain development. (2021, August 11). Cedars. https://cedarskids.org/news/news.html/article/2021/08/11/hold-me-close-physical-touch-and-brain-development

Homes, R. (n.d.). *3 powerful reasons why family traditions matter.* Brunswick Crossing. https://www.brunswickcrossing.com/blog/3-powerful-reasons-why-family-traditions-matter#:

Horsager-Boehrer, R. (2015, May 26). *"Baby blues" or postpartum depression?* UT Southwestern Medical Center. https://utswmed.org/medblog/postpartum-depression/

Horsager-Boehrer, R. (2021, August 17). *1 in 10 dads experience postpartum depression, anxiety: how to spot the signs.* UT Southwestern Medical Center. https://utswmed.org/medblog/paternal-postpartum-depression/

Huerta, D. (2020, September 1). *Adaptability — an essential parenting trait.* Focus on the Family. https://www.focusonthefamily.com/parenting/adaptability-an-essential-parenting-trait/

The importance of a father in a child's life. (2018, August 7). Pediatric Associates of Franklin. https://www.pediatricsoffranklin.com/resources-and-educa tion/pediatric-care/the-importance-of-a-father-in-a-childs-life/

The importance of mindful parenting. (2018, January 10). The Brain Workshop. https://www.thebrainworkshop.com/blog/the-importance-of-mindful- parenting/

The importance of schedules and routines. (2020, June 1). Head Start | Early Childhood Learning & Knowledge Center. https://eclkc.ohs.acf.hhs.gov/ about-us/article/importance-schedules-routines#:

It's normal! Understanding & overcoming overwhelming emotions as a new dad. (2023, February 3). Dad Central. https://dadcentral.ca/its-normal-under standing-overcoming-overwhelming-emotions-as-a-new-dad/

Jill. (2018, September 13). *Positive thinking day journal prompts.* Journal Buddies. https://www.journalbuddies.com/journal-prompts-writing- ideas/positive-thinking-day/

Jones, S. (2016, May 13). *Quantity of quality time.* Parent Cue. https://thepar entcue.org/quantity-of-quality-times/

Jones, S. J. (n.d.). *Why daddy should read the bedtime story.* King's Christian College. https://blog.kingscollege.qld.edu.au/why-daddy-should-read- the-bedtime-story

Kangaroo care. (2020, June 29). Cleveland Clinic. https://my.clevelandclinic. org/health/treatments/12578-kangaroo-care

Mackay, H. (n.d.). *Curiosity is one of nature's greatest gifts.* Des Moines Register. https://eu.desmoinesregister.com/story/money/business/columnists/ 2016/06/01/harvey-mackay-curiosity-one-natures-greatest-gifts/ 84940164/#:

Mae, E. (2023, June 18). *10 fatherhood reflections: thought-provoking dad journal prompts.* Coloring Folder. https://coloringfolder.com/dad-journal-prompts/

Majendie, C. (n.d.). *Baby's sleep routine: a father's role.* Naturalmat. https://natu ralmat.co.uk/blogs/news/baby-s-sleep-routine-a-father-s-role#:

Maltese, J. (2015, November 4). Your child's brain and healthy development. *Child Development Institute.* https://cdikids.org/child-development/brain- awareness-week-your-childs-healthy-growth/

Marcoux, H. (2017, October 23). *New parents lose 44 days of sleep during the first year of baby's life.* Motherly. https://www.mother.ly/parenting/real-sleep- stories-from-real-mamas/lost-sleep-baby-first-year/

McGinn, A. (2019, March 12). *Six sleep tips for new dads.* Good Night Sleep

Site. https://goodnightsleepsite.com/2019/03/12/sleep-tips-for-new-dads/

McIlroy, T. (2019, July 12). *Understanding the emotional needs of a child: 25 tips for parents.* Empowered Parents. https://empoweredparents.co/emotional-needs-of-a-child/

McKay, B., & McKay, K. (2010, February 22). *8 interesting (and insane) male rites of passages from around the world.* The Art of Manliness. https://www.artof manliness.com/character/behavior/male-rites-of-passage-from-around-the-world/

Meet children's needs as they change over time. (2023, May 19). Information Commissioner's Office. https://ico.org.uk/for-organisations/uk-gdpr-guidance-and-resources/designing-products-that-protect-privacy/chil drens-code-design-guidance/meet-children-s-needs-as-they-change-over-time/

Mental health and the new father. (n.d.). Mental Health America. https://mhana tional.org/mental-health-and-new-father

Migala, J. (2023, August 18). *8 permanent body changes after pregnancy.* Health. https://www.health.com/condition/pregnancy/body-changes-post-pregnancy

Mulvania, P. (2020, September 18). *The importance of active listening.* Gift of Life Institute. https://www.giftoflifeinstitute.org/the-importance-of-active-listening/

Mustering motivation. (2015). *British Dental Journal, 218*(8), 442–443. https://doi.org/10.1038/sj.bdj.2015.309

Nedovic, S. (2018, June 22). *Reading and storytelling with babies and children.* Raisingchildren.net.au. https://raisingchildren.net.au/babies/play-learn ing/literacy-reading-stories/reading-storytelling

New dad anxiety - how to overcome the fear of fatherhood. (2023, January 20). Dad University. https://www.daduniversity.com/blog/new-dad-anxiety-how-to-overcome-the-fear-of-fatherhood#:

New dads and partners: how your involvement matters. (2023, June 16). Healthy Children. https://www.healthychildren.org/English/ages-stages/baby/Pages/A-Special-Message-to-Fathers.aspx

Olsson, R. (2022, July 7). *Why is my partner jealous of the new baby?* Banner Health. https://www.bannerhealth.com/healthcareblog/advise-me/how-a-new-baby-can-trigger-jealousy-in-a-relationship

Overcoming fear. (n.d.). Good Therapy. https://www.goodtherapy.org/learn-about-therapy/issues/fear/overcome

Pacheco, D., & Snyder, C. (2021, June 9). *Understanding sleep deprivation and new parenthood.* Sleep Foundation. https://www.sleepfoundation.org/sleep-deprivation/parents

Pedersen, S. C., Maindal, H. T., & Ryom, K. (2021). "I wanted to be there as a father, but I couldn't": A qualitative study of fathers' experiences of post-partum depression and their help-seeking behavior. *American Journal of Men's Health,* *15*(3), 155798832110243. https://doi.org/10.1177/15579883211024375

Peek a boo. (2017, July 12). Parent Trust. https://www.parenttrust.org/2017/07/12/peek-a-boo/

Perry, E. (2022, August 25). *How to set boundaries at work: a personal guide to drawing the line.* Better Up. https://www.betterup.com/blog/how-to-set-boundaries-at-work

Philip, S. (2019, November 15). *Change is inevitable; growth is optional.* Linkedin. https://www.linkedin.com/pulse/change-inevitable-growth-optional-sneha-philip/

Positive thinking: activity for children, teenagers, and parents. (2022, November 16). Raisingchildren.net.au. https://raisingchildren.net.au/guides/activity-guides/wellbeing/positive-thinking

Prenatal care: the importance of prenatal education. (2022, March 30). Rosh Maternal & Fetal Medicine. https://roshmfm.com/prenatal-care-the-importance-of-prenatal-education/#:

Prichep, D. (2017, June 18). *This father's day, remembering a time when dads weren't welcome in delivery rooms.* NPR. https://www.npr.org/sections/health-shots/2017/06/18/532921305/this-fathers-day-remembering-a-time-when-dads-werent-welcome-in-delivery-rooms

Puzo, M. (n.d.). *Mario Puzo quotes.* Good Reads. https://www.goodreads.com/quotes/475769-the-strength-of-a-family-like-the-strength-of-an

Rampton, J. (2019, July 26). *15 ways to better manage your work-life balance as a parent and entrepreneur.* Entrepreneur. https://www.entrepreneur.com/living/15-ways-to-better-manage-your-work-life-balance-as-a-parent/337297

Role of the father-to-be in a healthy pregnancy. (2023, September 15). Health Hub. https://www.healthhub.sg/live-healthy/pregnancy-role-of-the-father-to-be

Roopnarine, J. L., & Yildirim, E. D. (2016, February). *Fathering in diverse cultural contexts: an emerging picture. Overall commentary on fathering.* Encyclopedia on Early Childhood Development. https://www.child-ency clopedia.com/father-paternity/according-experts/fathering-diverse-cultural-contexts-emerging-picture-overall

Sample, I. (2014, February 14). *Talking to babies boosts their brain power, studies show.* The Guardian. https://www.theguardian.com/science/2014/feb/14/talking-to-babies-brain-power-language

Satyavasan, C. (2021, May 4). *Why curiosity is an important quality in helping children learn and plan new ideas.* Parent Circle. https://www.parentcircle.com/why-curiosity-is-important-in-children/article

Schwahn, L. (2023, September 6). *Free budget planner: tips for getting started.* NerdWallet. https://www.nerdwallet.com/article/finance/budget-worksheet

Scroggs, L. (2023). *Time blocking.* Todoist. https://todoist.com/productivity-methods/time-blocking

Shaelyn. (2023, June 13). *Not your typical dad: how modern dads break stereotypes.* Familius. https://www.familius.com/not-your-typical-dad-how-modern-dads-break-stereotypes/

Sheldon, R. (2022, September). *What is the Pomodoro technique?* WhatIs.com. https://www.techtarget.com/whatis/definition/pomodoro-technique#:

Shwalb, D. W., & Shwalb, B. J. (2014). Fatherhood in Brazil, Bangladesh, Russia, Japan, and Australia. *Online Readings in Psychology and Culture, 6*(3). https://doi.org/10.9707/2307-0919.1125

Singh, R., Zapata, M., & Morris, A. S. (2018, November 1). *Talk, read and sing with your child every day.* Oklahoma State University. https://extension.okstate.edu/fact-sheets/talk-read-and-sing-with-your-child-every-day.html#:

16 family tradition ideas to start with your kids. (2023, August 7). Southern Living. https://www.southernliving.com/culture/family-tradition-ideas

Smith, S. (2017a, July 25). *10 effective techniques for communication for couples.* Marriage.com. https://www.marriage.com/advice/communication/tips-for-effective-communication-between-couples/

Smith, S. (2017b, November 13). *Top 10 effective communication techniques for couples.* PsychAlive. https://www.psychalive.org/top-10-effective-communication-techniques-couples/

Speech therapy: How to track my toddler's first words. (2015, November 12). My

Toddler Talks. https://www.mytoddlertalks.com/kims-blog/speech-ther apy-how-to-track-my-toddlers-first-words

Sutton, J. (2019, January 3). *What is resilience and why is it important to bounce back?* Positive Psychology. https://positivepsychology.com/what-is-resilience/#:

Talley, L. (2017). *First-time fathers' perspectives on pregnancy, birth, and fatherhood.* Walden University. https://core.ac.uk/download/pdf/147840818.pdf

10 ways to boost your personal resilience and better cope with stress. (2022). Zurich. https://www.zurich.com/en/media/magazine/2021/10-steps-that-will-increase-your-personal-resilience

25 things to do when preparing for fatherhood. (2022, August 22). Pampers. https://www.pampers.com/en-us/pregnancy/preparing-for-your-new-baby/article/preparing-for-fatherhood

29 time management templates and examples to enhance efficiency. (2022, December 17). Asana. https://asana.com/resources/time-management-templates

Vehrs, S. (2020, December 29). *25 powerful birth affirmations for dads.* She Births Bravely. https://shebirthsbravely.com/birth-affirmations-for-dads/

Vidakovic, F. (2023, March 8). *50 journal prompts for relationships – to help nurture your love.* Inspiring Life. https://www.inspiringmomlife.com/jour nal-prompts-for-relationships/

What bodily changes can you expect during pregnancy? (2012). Healthline. https://www.healthline.com/health/pregnancy/bodily-changes-during

Why fatherhood engagement matters. (2017, May 1). Children's Bureau. https://www.all4kids.org/news/blog/why-fatherhood-engagement-matters/#:

Why hire a financial advisor. (2023, May 24). Fidelity. https://www.fidelity.com/viewpoints/investing-ideas/financial-advisor-cost#:

Why play is important. (2019, June 24). Raisingchildren.net.au. https://rais ingchildren.net.au/newborns/play-learning/play-ideas/why-play-is-important

Wirth, J. (2023, April 9). *35 positive affirmations to empower your child.* Parents. https://www.parents.com/kids/health/childrens-mental-health/32posi tive-affirmations-for-kids-and-why-theyre-so-important/

Wisner, W. (2021, June 14). *How to support your partner during pregnancy.* Verywell Family. https://www.verywellfamily.com/partner-support-during-pregnancy-4797874

Work-life balance: tips for you and your family. (2021, July 27). Raisingchildren.net.au. https://raisingchildren.net.au/grown-ups/work-child-care/worklife-balance/work-life-balance#:

Your relationship after having a baby: dads' perspective. (2020, December 10). National Childbirth Trust. https://www.nct.org.uk/life-parent/your-relationship-couple/relationship-changes/your-relationship-after-having-baby-dads-perspective

www.ingramcontent.com/pod-product-compliance
Lightning Source LLC
Chambersburg PA
CBHW021643120626
46545CB00002B/677